CRAZY
QUILT

When the Pennsylvania Germans came in and got land,
that was it.
No second west for them. They built
stone houses and barns to last. A common saying,
"Three movings is one burning," meaning
the same amount of damage.
They stayed where they stopped.
The children stayed, too. If away,
they suffered from heemweh, *"home longing."*

From "Their Temperament" by Millen Brand, *Local Lives: Poems About the Pennsylvania Dutch* (New York: Clarkson N. Potter, Inc., 1975; distributed by Crown Publishers)

CRAZY QUILT

Pieces of a Mennonite Life

Cynthia Yoder

Foreword by
John L. Ruth

Diary Excerpts by
Elizabeth Kulp Yoder

Illustrations by
Juanita Yoder Kauffman

DreamSeeker Books
TELFORD, PENNSYLVANIA

an imprint of
Cascadia Publishing House

Copublished with
Herald Press
Scottdale, Pennsylvania

Cascadia Publishing House orders, information, reprint permissions:
contact@CascadiaPublishingHouse.com
1-215-723-9125
126 Klingerman Road, Telford PA 18969
www.CascadiaPublishingHouse.com

Crazy Quilt
Copyright © 2003 by Cascadia Publishing House.
Telford, PA 18969
All rights reserved
DreamSeeker Books is an imprint of Cascadia Publishing House.
Copublished with Herald Press, Scottdale, PA
Library of Congress Catalog Number: 2003049384
ISBN: 1-931038-14-7
Printed in Canada by Pandora Press
Book design by Cascadia Publishing House
Illustrations by Juanita Yoder Kauffman
Cover design by Gwen M. Stamm

The paper used in this publication is recycled and meets the
minimum requirements of American National Standard for Information Sciences—
Permanence of Paper for Printed Library Materials, ANSI Z39.48-1984.1984

Grateful acknowledgment is made to Jonathan Brand for permission to reprint
the page 2 excerpt from the poem, "Their Temperament," by Millen Brand.

The text of the prayer shown on p. 172 entered Mennonite homes via the oral tradition but has a literary tradition in *Sing and Rejoice* (Scottdale, Pa.: Herald Press,
1979), no. 131, which also deserves recognition.

Disclaimer: Although this is a work of nonfiction,
a few names have been changed.

Library of Congress Cataloguing-in-Publication Data
Yoder, Cynthia, 1966-
    Crazy Quilt : pieces of a Mennonite life / Cynthia Yoder ; foreword by
John L. Ruth ; diary excerpts by Elizabeth Kulp Yoder ; illustrations by
Juanita Yoder Kauffman.
        p.cm.
    ISBN 1-931038-14-7 (trade pbk. : alk paper)
        1. Yoder, Cynthia, 1966. 2 Mennonites--United States--Biography. I. Title.

E184.M45Y626 2003
289.7'092--dc22
[B]

2003049384

11 10 09 08 07 06 05 04   10 9 8 7 6 5 4 3

For my parents,
Ray and Edna (Mack) Yoder and
for Jonathan

Contents

Foreword

*H*ere we have four stories woven as one: a quest for home; a memoir; the "romance" of a grandparental couple; and the story of how their stories come together. Each thread has color and texture.

During the writing, the memoir strand has moved from subtext to foreground. The granddaughter's quest for a writer's voice enlarges into a search for identity. Along the way, her urgent curiosity must invent some of its own strategy. The two unpretentious people who have the part of her story she most hungers for must be approached with tender skill amid the fragility of their closing days.

The author speaks for a post-Boomer generation at home with anomie and an urgent sense that something its roots need is passing. She represents a diaspora, from Boston to San Diego and beyond, of grandchildren with Mennonite memory both disturbing and nostalgic. Her specific memory is of a flavorful southeastern Pennsylvania village from which some gravitate to New York City, while others move in the exactly opposite path. Each community, the author realizes, has its sacred.

Of course Mennonites removed from their roots have no corner on post-rural hunger for material—soil, subsoil, primal aromas. In any culture, the haunting taste of a food known in childhood, as the tea-soaked madeleine biscuit for Proust, can trigger a sudden overwhelming connection between adult hunger and the primal sensation of felicity. Here a granddaughter's relish of her grandmother's savory "Dutch Goose," or her grandfather's quaint, tinkering humor, take her toward inner reconciliation. Humble familial "patterns," she muses, "have the potential to comfort."

Importantly, the world-acquainted granddaughter has the patience to let the grandparents' meek voices emerge without a heavy overlay of her own. The latter can wait its turn. After all, she does not instantly understand everything she hears. She does not recognize—or at least does not note—the Scriptures and hymns echoing in the cadences she treasures from her grandfather. Growing up between worlds has not supplied that local, verbal ambiance. A ten-generation, intramural Mennonite past is little preparation for a nuanced encounter with generic American culture, with its individualism, its marriages gone awry, its loneliness, its non-specificity of memory.

For that matter, Baby Boomers of all cultures have not "heard many of the old stories"; haven't heard a great-grandfather's pungent sermons over the riffling of a hundred Bible-leaves in response to his shouted references; haven't read their great-grandmothers' diaries; haven't absorbed, in a mood beyond amusement, accents and phrases that used to epitomize their people's seriousness. Thus the present writer, who has known emptiness, and her grandparents, who have not, don't have the same vocabulary. But she is recapturing something; she finds charm in their archaic expressions. Eliminating the screen of her own hastiness by using a tape recorder, she sifts respectfully among their modest mantras of "Well," and "I guess."

Moving past pity for the child in ourselves that communal pressure sometimes frightens into abortive confessions and affirmations, the author likewise accepts the shock, common to middle age, of finding herself repeating parental manners.

Once free to listen to the story she seeks, she finds she can stroke the crazy quilt of familial patterns with affection.

Her grandparents' story is told. As hers is still unfolding, she speaks of the Buddha and a longing for—even a quick taste of—nirvana. While such terms are foreign to her devout grandfather, his laconic account of his own peace-bringing glimpses into "the heavenlies" brings her a twinge of connection. She senses that there is something more than zero left of her own childhood faith. Hearing trans-generational voices with an acuity that vagueness had dulled, she senses more than dogma and empty transition in her heritage. Under the brown leaves her grandmother stirs in the late fall there are bright red berries.

—*John L. Ruth*
  Vernfield, Pennsylvania

Author's Preface: The Beginning

The daffodils on Broadway were glowing under the street-lamps, and the buds auditioned for their roles on the trees of Riverside Park. In spring in New York City, the fauna bloom along with the flora. People, in as much variety as their vegetable counterparts, burst out of their hovels onto the sidewalks and promenades to recharge with solar vitamin D. They roller blade like fast ants, or saunter down the avenues with glances into bodegas (where the lotto is up to $2 million). They carry their boom boxes on their shoulders like they're showing off a young child.

Spring is usually my favorite time of year—it is the playground of seasons. But this spring, I was sitting on a mood swing that was no longer swinging.

I was stuck, and even though I was twenty-something, I'd forgotten how to pump.

During the three years I'd been living in New York since college, I'd accepted a low-grade emotional burn as a normal part of getting through the day. On this blooming night in spring, however, the word *normal* no longer seemed to apply. Normal, in fact, had gone out on a long walk without saying when she'd be back. I was not out at the movies or enjoying late-night ice cream. I was lying flat on my back in bed, holding onto my thin cotton sheets, trying to make sense of a filmy gray presence that was hovering near the ceiling above me.

At the time, I believed in presences no more than I believed in an honest politician. But belief has a way of morphing when a blob hovers over you like an unbidden marketing call from the beyond. The thing was undulating and would not go away, no matter how I turned my head or blinked my eyes, or told myself I was making this up. The thing had no form except that it rolled like ocean water and was just big enough (I noticed) for me to disappear into it, if that had been its choice.

I was so drenched with fear I didn't think to wake my husband, who was deep in sleep beside me. The reference points we had for this kind of phenomenon were unacceptable: (1) demon possession; or (2) madness. I closed my eyes and pressed myself against Jonathan, hoping—the way I did as a child climbing in next to my mother in bed—that this would somehow save me from annihilation.

When I woke in the morning, the sun was up, the pigeons on the fire escape were squabbling, and the apparition was gone. I didn't tell anyone what had happened, planning to keep my sanity intact by force of will.

But morose things began to happen in great abundance that springtime, causing me to question my own power over my sanity. I started seeing sinister faces—unwelcome faeries— in squished gum or smeared dirt on the floor of subway trains. I saw images of my dismembered body flashing in front of me on the platform while I awaited the train to go to work. I dreaded sleep, because it was a gateway into a field of gruesome nightmares. And like many people who are depressed, I did everything I could to avoid being alone.

I told myself I was no Anna Karenina—I'd never throw myself in front of a train. But I wasn't sure that my rational self would have the last say on that. I tried distraction. I went to work, had coffee with friends, went out dancing, stayed up late. But it is hard to feel normal when it seems like your own mind is out to get you, and it's only a matter of time until it succeeds. It is even harder to be a good partner to someone else.

If, like me, you were married, or had a lover, you might begin to suspect that because he is deeply connected to you, and you are very ill, he might have your same disease. Or worse, that he is the one who gave it to you in the first place. I didn't stick around long enough to find out whether either was true. In late spring, I told Jonathan that I didn't know if I loved him anymore. We broke glasses and plates in a last ditch effort to impress each other with emotion, but after two weeks I packed up my clothes and walked out on my marriage of two brief years. I was going to live with my friend Eleanor downtown.

Sense can hardly ever be made out of relationships ending. Whether it happens slowly, over the course of a lifetime, or all of a sudden, like a thunderstorm in the month of May, there remains on your mental curb a scuffed suitcase full of disbelief. First there was love and a bonfire of hormones. Then there was something else—not apathy, not lack of feeling—just an absence of love, or the absence of love the way you expected it to behave. An empty stage, when you were expecting a play.

Eleanor is a poet and movie reviewer whom I'd met at a writing workshop at Columbia University. She's tall with a sturdy stature and irreverent humor that steadied me while I vomited up my marriage. She lived in Little Italy near Chinatown, and so when I got back to the place where I was eating more than smoking, I filled up on Chinese cabbage and tofu and put fat back on my bones with Italian cheesecake.

After a couple of weeks, though, it became evident that my illness had moved all of its belongings downtown with me, so I began to think out loud with Eleanor and my mother about what I could do to make myself happy again.

One, I could stay with Eleanor and laugh myself back to health, except that I had neglected to fulfill the necessary coursework to renew my elementary school teaching certificate, and so had no job lined up for fall. Two, I could leave the city and start over again. One night on the phone with my mother, I revisited a very impractical idea that I'd had the year before. I could head home and collect stories from my Pennsylvania Dutch Mennonite family.

"That sounds workable," Mom said, always the optimist, bouncy as her brown bob. The fact that I had just derailed myself from my career track didn't seem to phase her.

"I imagine one of the aunts and uncles might be willing to rent out a room—for a fair rate," she said. I could see the wheel in her blue sky turning. I talked about staying with her parents, who lived on a farm north of Philadelphia. I had spent loads of time on the farm as a child, and envisioned lying in a haystack, writing out my stories, the cows grumbling in the barn below. But my grandmother was suffering her own depression, and my mother and I agreed it would be too confusing.

When Mom called back later and said she'd found an arrangement for living near my dad's parents, I felt that perhaps a god was looking out for me after all: her name was Mom. I would stay with my dad's twin, Roy, and his wife Sandi, who lived next door to my grandparents, Henry and Betts Yoder, on Kulp Hill. My aunt and uncle had a basement apartment that was empty, and they were willing to accommodate me.

I realize hanging out with one's family can actually tip a wobbling sanity in the wrong direction. But I felt drawn to what I suspected was a simpler life than the one I'd been living in New York. Henry and Betts, now in their early eighties, came from generations of Mennonites who saw themselves as separate from the world and so took their changes slowly. I, on the other hand, had stripped off my childhood culture in quick teenage gestures. I was all new, not given to looking back at old ways and old times. Perhaps that's why my grandparents' lives intrigued me so much. Their lives were based on roots, while my life was based on change. The heritage I had abandoned was as solid as the Hill my family had come to so many years ago, their belongings strapped to a horse-drawn wagon.

So I went, click-click, like Dorothy in her ruby slippers. Jonathan and I broke down our Upper West Side apartment, sold our random furnishings to neighboring Columbia University students, and boxed up the rest for storage. He went to live with friends. I set up shop in Bally, Pennsylvania, to tether myself to the fat root of my family and to the black soil of Kulp Hill.

Of course, as the saying goes, you can't truly go home again. Home is simply a memory, a place that no longer exists in the real world after you've been away for a long time. To truly go home would be to return to what you were before you left, to relinquish everything you've become. But you can try to return. Just as you can try anything. You can return with a little of you, just that teeny part that agrees to go. Maybe I would learn something I'd forgotten, or a thing not learned well enough the first time around. I told my friends it was just for a summer, so that I could write poetry. But I was more desperate than that.

At first, I felt very awkward, a withered specimen from New York, wearing too much black and smoking in stolen moments, late at night, on the driveway. I kept a pint of Wild Turkey I'd brought from New York in my desk drawer, which I sipped late at night after everyone else was in bed. When a week passed, and the bottle was empty, I drove to the local pizza joint and tossed it into the dumpster. I didn't plan on replacing it. I was going to do what one of my friends called "52-card pick-up with your life." I was going to change my life all over again.

CRAZY QUILT

Gott ist die Liebe.

No. 210.

AUG. RISCHE.   Volksweise.

1. Gott ist die Lie = be, Läßt mich er = lö = sen; Gott ist die Lie = be, Er
2. Ich lag in Banden Der schnö=den Sün=den; Ich lag in Ban=den Und
3. Je = sus, mein Hei=land, Gab sich zum O = pfer; Je = sus, mein Heiland, Büßt

Chor.

liebt auch mich.
konnt' nicht los. } Drum sag' ich
mei = ne Schuld. }

ist die Lie = be, Er liebt auch

Chapter 1

When I Was a Boy

*T*here wasn't much to do in Bally. I jogged up Kulp Hill—or Crow Hill, as some call it—past houses nested in the woods, many of them Kulps, from Betts' extended family. A farm stood at the crest with a chicken house, a few scarecrows out in the fields, and a lone black dog. Coming down another road, I passed a farm in a green valley peppered with white sheep. I jogged down through town, past the small white Catholic church, then corn and alfalfa fields one after another.

On one of my first days on the Hill, I walked along the edge of a small farm behind my grandparents place. The barn was so close to the road you could almost reach out and touch the wood that showed through the worn red paint. A metal plow, old and rusted, posed in tufts of grass. I eventually came to a stream and took off my shoes to go barefoot in the shallow water. The stones were slippery with moss, and the cold water startled my feet. A boulder jutted out from the middle of the stream, and sun swirled around on top like a strobe. I climbed up and sat down. I had spent many days as a child on rocks and boulders, wandering in streams, and playing in the woods. I felt something shift in me as I relaxed now -on this boulder that was so unmovable, so unchanged—so unlike myself. My body had felt tense and worn, but there on the boulder, part of me slowly began to loosen, like crumbling shale. I wanted to be part of something known again. I wanted to be home, though I had no idea what that was.

◆

History has a way of sucking at your feet, a mud that you'd like to wash off, except that something in the scent of it makes you feel proud and certain. Or proud and crazy. I had a love-hate relationship with the Mennonites. They were my family; they were my centuries-old roots. But I blamed them for the rules that made me feel separate from my friends at school, and now, as an adult, separate from the culture around me. I grew up as one of the few Mennonites in a non-Mennonite town. My friends, my neighborhood playmates, almost everyone I related to as a child was "the world"— the people I supposedly was separate from.

I couldn't watch their cartoons, listen to their music, dance at their school dances, or wear their groovy halter tops. I couldn't go see "Star Wars" or go to the mall on Sundays. I was a Mennonite minister's daughter, living by a set of rules only my family followed. But this "world" I was supposed to avoid was always knocking on my back door, asking if I wanted to come out and play. How could I be separate from my friends?

When Jonathan and I met in college, we were instant friends; we were like Tang. He wore earrings and wrote poetry. He was so bicultural—his parents were Mennonite missionaries to Africa—that he made me feel normal. When we moved to New York together after college, we flocked with other odd birds—a blues guitarist, a handful of poets, other ex-Mennonites. We went to drag queen parties, drank whiskey, did yoga, and wrote off a God who would judge us for any of it.

But it was my habit to feel separate from my friends, and I started feeling separate from Jonathan, too. I thought that if people really got to know me, they wouldn't understand me at all. When two of my girlfriends that year each—one week after the next—ended up at the hospital for cutting their wrists, I visited them, took them books, and wished I were so brave. I tried to envision cutting my own wrists but minutes later would be totally paranoid paring an apple, afraid that my knife would slip and I'd kill myself accidentally. When I packed my bags for the Hill, I was desperate for some sense of inner balance. But I had no language to talk about this. I didn't even think such a thing was possible for me. So I just listened.

◆

Henry closed his copy of *Popular Mechanics* and lowered it to his lap. He looked reticent, unsure of our arrangement. Betts was crocheting. Her white lace doily was almost complete and would be added to the batch she'd offer the family at Christmas. Betts' recliner, and the green scratchy sofa where I sat— Betts called it the davenport—faced the bay window, where we could look out past a flower garden, a small shed, and a vegetable garden to the woods. Theirs was a small apartment in the bottom of Betts' sister Ruth's house. The living room was divided from the dining room by the davenport, and the dining room from the kitchen by a short inlet of sink and cabinets.

The black-eyed Susans by the driveway were nodding in a summer breeze. Henry was tapping his fingertips together. When Henry spoke, it was usually after not talking for a long time, or after much cajoling from Betts. He sat in his worn, brown recliner, his feet resting on the floor, his hands folded over his ample abdomen. His crane-white hair was brushed neatly back. He wore a long-sleeved shirt buttoned at his neck and tucked into his trousers. On his feet were white stockings that went up to his knees, and corduroy slippers. When he

---

Diary, Jan. 1, 1933. This evening we were at Bible Meeting at Schantz's. This book was a birthday present from my Hubby. *Betts' Diary*, Bally, Pennsylvania

began answering my questions, he spoke slowly and in a thin, underused voice.

"I didn't speak English before the first grade," he said, clearing his throat and moving his swivel chair slightly to the left then back again. "At home, we spoke Pennsylvania Dutch. Church was in German, but in school, they didn't allow the children to speak Pennsylvania Dutch."

"What happened if you did?" I asked, speaking softly to match his voice. I was in chameleon mode, trying to fade in with the davenport, hoping that in erasing myself, I would have a better chance of becoming something new.

"If you spoke it," he replied, "you were reprimanded. The teacher put you into a corner, or she made you stay in at recess. You didn't speak it again. I learned English quick."

"And church, too, you said, was in German," Betts urged.

By the tone of her question, I could tell she was irritated at the uncertain pace of Henry's words, his frail voice. She fingered the neckline of her floral-print polyester dress. Betts was on the short side, her graying hair thinning with age, but she had a force within her, a kind of chutzpah that gave her the air of a much larger and commanding presence.

I was taking notes with pen and paper, wishing I knew shorthand. I asked lots of questions, feeling out of place, a writer looking for a story that would save me, among a family who believed salvation happens by asking Jesus into your heart. I suspected it wasn't that simple, but I didn't have anything better to show—I was a droopy and brown-spotted transplant, while my grandparents seemed to be thriving on Miracle Grow.

"The church services, they were conducted in high German," Henry said, clearing his voice. "The men were on one side, and the women on the other, not together like they do now. And you knew what was going to happen each Sunday. You'd sing two songs, in four parts, then there'd be the sermon. And then the deacon would give testimony. He'd say, 'I can say yea and amen to what the brother has said.'"

Betts interrupted, "If they talked high German, how would the Pennsylvania Dutch understand?"

High German, from the highlands of Germany, was different than Plat Deutsch, the lowland dialect of the Pennsylvania Germans. I understood neither, despite a summer spent at Jena Universitat.

"You didn't," Henry answered with a dry laugh, "Just a few words."

◆

Language is the thread that weaves people together, in love, in hate, or in some combination of the two. Although I grew up speaking English, sometimes it felt like I had no language. Because I wasn't allowed to watch cartoons or listen to pop music, I had no idea what my friends were talking about most of the time. With nothing to contribute in the way of Tom and Jerry scenarios or Cher worship, I sat and listened, laughed when my friends laughed, and wished I could stow away to one of their houses for the rest of my childhood. If we had been talking about the Bible, I would have had the language. But we weren't. We were talking about Erik Estrada's butt.

I craved going to friends' houses so I could get a glimpse into this forbidden universe. But when I watched "Planet of the Apes" at my best friend's house, or held hands in a nine-year-old birthday party attempt at a séance, I knew there might be eternal consequences for me. My great-grandfather, Elias W. Kulp, a Mennonite evangelist, repeatedly said that he would not die before the Lord returned. Every time we visited him at the Souderton Mennonite Home, he'd shake his blue-veined

> Jan. 12, 1933. I did a lot of mending today. I cooked 12 lb. mush for Henry to sell on his route. I also baked five medium size shoo-fly cakes to sell if he can. Henry was working for [brother-in-law] Arland today. This eve. they pick chickens for market.

hand and reiterate this claim. For me, this meant that unless my great-grandfather lived well beyond the age of 100, Jesus was probably going to return to judge the living and the dead before my tenth birthday. Hopefully it wouldn't happen while I was trying to play cool with my friends.

◆

"Ach, there's another thing," Betts said, frowning and waving her hand as if to shoo away a fly. "If the parents couldn't hardly afford to take care of their children, feed and clothe them, they were put out on a farm. Your brother Norman," she said to Henry, "he was only eight when he was sent. Imagine. He said he had terrible homesickness. When you were hired out to the Huber family in Spring City, you were fourteen."

Henry responded slowly. "Yes, I was fourteen then."

"Tell how far you'd go." Betts tried to push him beyond his halting answer.

Pointing to the palm of his hand as a map, my grandfather dutifully showed the route.

"I'd go from Allentown to Norristown by trolley," he said. "In Norristown, I'd get the train to Spring City. That was my way of going. But not often. I didn't have the fare money."

"Why were you hired out?" I asked. This detail from Henry's childhood was known among my family members, but the why of it was never part of the story, an unplowed row at the edge of the field.

Henry replied, "I helped the Hubers on their farm—chores and such. They called it the little hire."

"You always said you were there for your keep—for room and board," Betts said, leaning toward him, her elbow on her armrest. She could barely contain herself. Now that we had him talking, she couldn't get enough.

"Your parents were so poor they couldn't afford to feed you?" I asked, incredulously. I put down my pen, not wanting Henry to be scared by the act of recording.

"I don't know," Betts said, looking down at the floor.

"I guess that was it," Henry replied, noncommittal, again swiveling his chair slightly. "My pop drove a baker's route, and he was getting ten dollars a week, plus raised goods. Raised goods included bread."

"Buns," Betts added.

"No," Henry countered. "Buns were a luxury. At any rate, he was getting ten dollars a week. And I was one extra to feed. I guess that's what it was."

"Well, if you could feed one child off a loaf, you could feed two," Betts snapped.

She didn't take stock in his story.

Turning to me, she confided, "With the stepmother, it didn't go so well. She favored her own girls."

I looked at Henry. He was tapping his fingers against the armrests of his chair. Henry's mother had died seven days after he was born, after complications from childbirth. Several years later, his father had married, and they had two girls of their own. I'd never heard that they were poor. Struggling, yes, but not poor. Henry didn't say a word.

"We didn't have bad feelings for my sisters," he said, finally. "We always called them sisters. In any case, you weren't paid as a hired boy. You'd work on the farm for room and board."

"Well, tell what all you'd do," Betts pressed, still miffed from the stepmother story.

"It was my job to curry the horses and get them ready for the day's work. And milk the cow."

"You said you got up at four in the morning," Betts prompted.

Henry paused, swiveling his chair, "Six would be the time for the milk train, it was called, to leave for Philadelphia."

Jan. 13, 1933. Henry was on his route in Allentown. He sold four of the cakes I baked at 15 c. each.

"Wasn't it dark by then?" Betts asked. She should have been a journalist.

"Sure," Henry said, rubbing his fingers over his chin.

"After that we had to throw the hay down, and feed them grain. Hubers had a boy about my age . . . "

"What'd he do?" Betts asked sharply, "Stay in bed?"

I sided with Betts. I thought Henry was too forgiving. On the other hand, I admired his lack of bitterness, his willingness to look at what happened without judgment—it was simply what happened.

Henry answered plainly, "I guess he'd start feeding the cows."

After this talk, I decided they would have to take turns for Henry to tell a story without interruption. When Betts became excited, she was very verbose, and Henry deferred to her. So a few days later when we came together again, I asked if we could agree on one rule: Betts would wait quietly while Henry spoke, and vice versa. This made Betts laugh, but she cooperated.

This put Henry at ease. His voice relaxed.

"There was a harrow," Henry said, leaning forward a little in his chair. "Do you know what a harrow is?"

"No," I replied. My hand was getting writer's cramp almost before I began.

"The harrow slices the ground to prepare the field for planting," he explained. "They also had a roller. There was a seat on it. You'd sit on the roller to drive the horses. You'd sit about a foot from the blade of the harrow." He showed the amount of space with his hands. One foot.

I looked over at Betts, who returned my glance, her hands folded in her lap. She looked like an eager schoolgirl who wasn't getting called on. She put her hand over her mouth, smiling mischievously.

"Well, out at Hubers, I was taking the harrow through the field," Henry continued "The horses got scared. They were spry. I don't know why; they were spooked by something. Well, they took off, me behind. Straight through the field to the fence. I hung on. But I was scared. I prayed that if God let me live, I'd confess God's name Sunday in church. I'd serve God."

Henry's voice wavered. "The horses came toward the fence, turned, then they stopped. Just like that, they stopped. Sunday, I confessed God, like I'd said."

He paused to pull a white cotton handkerchief from his trouser pocket and wipe his eyes, which were teary.

"Now, I wonder," he continued, tucking away the hankie, "did I live up to that? Did I live up to what I'd promised?" I thought of a list of things: his volunteer work at the church, the conscientious way he raised his children, his love for Betts. I began to protest, but stopped. He wasn't looking for reassurances from me, a mortal, a faltering mortal at that. Henry was thinking about how he'd answer, standing at the Almighty's feet as he underwent a lifetime evaluation that would condemn him or save him from eternal fire.

The standards in my family were as high as the jetstream.

Henry stood up and walked to the kitchen. He came back with a plastic container full of hard pretzels and passed them around. Hard pretzels were a staple here. Something would be awry if you visited for more than ten minutes and weren't served pretzels.

But as Henry passed around the Tupperware container, I saw something strangely different about him. I'd been judging myself for not being able to live up to my family's standards. And here the patriarch himself wondered if he too failed the standard. I saw now that we were not all that different: We were two human beings, trying to catapult for the sky. When my

Mar. 11, 1933. I did my mending. Cleaned upstairs and boiled some soap this afternoon. First time I ever boiled soap. This eve. I did some sewing, made button holes in a suit for little J. Arland

grandfather lowered himself back into his chair slowly, I saw him as he was—an old man, with white hair, wondering about his life. I wanted to rush over and kiss him.

The bird in the cuckoo clock called twice, followed by the grandfather clock. Then it was the heirloom clock's turn. All of them were Henry's. He loved clocks as much as pretzels.

Henry's voice was strained from talking so long. He had to keep clearing his throat to get a solid sound.

"There was an epidemic then. Of influenza. On the farm, out at Hubers, all got sick but the boss and me. With everyone sick, there was no one to take care of the farm. So I quit the eighth grade to help take care of things."

Henry shifted in his chair. "I never went back to finish school after that. Why not? Why didn't I finish? Well, I guess there was a job for me in Allentown, so I didn't need to go back. Then I worked in a store in Allentown, for a man named Sam Osman. We were paid twenty-five dollars a week to start.

"We delivered milk—you see, most people had a milkman coming around. In those times, a grocery store would send a man out to sell groceries. And a farmer would come around and sell potatoes in the fall.

"But we were minors yet, and we gave all of our money to our parents. My brother Norman and I were allowed thirty-five cents a week for ourselves. With that, we bought our own gas. Later on, we could buy a car together—a Ford. That thirty-five cents had to last us for all our extras."

Betts leaned forward and said confidingly, "They had girl-friends to buy candy for."

Henry chuckled, mischief glittering in his eyes. He picked up the pretzel container and passed it around again.

"I used to buy Betts candy across town at a candy store," he said. "It was cheaper there; they had pieces. Lofts used to be my choice. Anyway, that way I worked until—well, all us boys worked until we were twenty-one, giving our earnings to our parents."

I typed up my notes from Henry's stories, thinking about him as a young boy, sent far from home for dubious reasons. He could have hated his family for that, but he didn't. He had suffered, and he had forgiven. That's what I wanted to learn. I carried my suffering around with me like a fifty-pound dead dog.

◆

Over the next few weeks, I organized my notes and did logistical things like searching for a cheap second-hand car, transferring my driver's license, and applying for auto insurance. On one sunny afternoon, in which I had absolutely nothing to do, I walked up the Hill, past my grandparents' house, and into the woods. The woods are usually a place where I feel most alive, a place where I feel part of something big and harmonious, and it smells good, too. I decided I would take the afternoon and wander aimlessly, be a raccoon for the day. I deliberately headed off the path and eventually came upon a grove of pine trees that had dropped a thick bed of needles into a clearing. The woods looked magical. The sun shone through the trees onto the needles, making them a reddish gold. I came closer, losing myself in the scent of the pines, the softness of the needles underfoot.

Then something caught my eye. It was a log rotting in the clearing, and as I looked closer, I saw that there was something different about the log. It had a face, and it wasn't a very nice face. It glared at me, its eyes red and condemning. I stared at it, the way, when you're driving, you stare at a lump on the road, hoping to see that it's garbage and not a dead animal. I was hoping it would change back to an ordinary log, but it was a defiant beast, staring at me just like the countless smudges and squished gum in the subway. The bad faeries, spirits, or what-

Mar. 31, 1933. I did some cleaning and made myself four Sunday coverings.[1]

ever they were, had followed me here. I turned and ran out of the woods, out onto the road. I kept running the half-mile back to my apartment. I tried to forget about it, chalking it up to an overactive imagination and a hefty dose of self-judgment. But it disturbed me; the thing had broken into my sanctuary.

♦

The next week, we resurrected Henry's father, Henry, Sr. I'd seen pictures of him, a portly grocer who buttered his pie and who died of heart disease in his sixties. It was comforting to me to talk about the dead. I didn't believe in life after death, except in a metaphorical way, through memory. So we played around in my kind of heaven—resurrecting ancestors through resurrecting their stories.

"My father was fairly strict," Henry said, fingering the corners of the magazine on his lap as he spoke.

My grandmother was in the kitchen, poking around in the cupboards for the makings of dinner.

"He taught us right and wrong. As a boy, we didn't play the same games as other children. And we didn't go to movies. For instance, my Aunt Emma bought us a croquet set, but she said, don't play it on Sundays, because she knew my father wouldn't approve. We never went to the Allentown fair. That was one of the places we just didn't attend. My father always said, 'Remember the Sabbath Day, to keep it holy.'

"I haven't been to a movie house. Well, maybe that's not accurate. I think one time my brothers and I had a small job, and we spent the money going to a movie house. But we never had a habit of going to the movies.

"My father was strict, as I say, but we didn't have Bible reading every day. After I was married and established our family, we had Bible reading and prayer every evening before bed."

Henry unclasped his fingers to tap them on his thighs. All of this talk of movies made me uncomfortable again. I felt if he really knew me, he would be disappointed. He was a man of keen principles and a sharp-edged morality. I was rather open-minded concerning morals, sort of hunt-and-peck as I went along. I wondered what he would say if he knew I'd been the one who left.

"I don't know if it was my father or my stepmother," Henry continued, "both of them did, I guess. They'd say, 'Look, I'm going to whip you. Go get a stick.' And then I'd go out to get a stick so they could use it to whip me. Of course, I had to use my own judgment as to which stick was suitable. So I didn't bring a piece of grass in, because that wouldn't have been accepted."

Henry was rubbing a cheek with his palm, "My father smoked cigars. At the church, they used to put their cigars on the window sill outside before they went in. After church they picked them up again and smoked the rest of the cigar.

"We had a spittoon in the church. One was behind the pulpit. Well, what is a spittoon for? How about the fellows who chewed tobacco? We got rid of spittoons during the George Brunk revival. After George Brunk came through, none of the tobacco was allowed anymore."

The George Brunk revival was a flame that spread through communities, keeping them spiritually and moralistically upright. My uncles and aunts talk about thousands of people crammed into tents with wood-chip flooring, singing hymns and listening to long, stirring sermons by the revivalist about the Holy Spirit. But there was always that motivating underside: *God will separate the wheat from the chaff! The wages of sin are death!* The revivals solidified conservatism among eastern Pennsylvania Mennonites for the next generation and more.

Oct. 13, 1933. Almost a month has elapsed since I wrote in here again. I was helping husk corn in my spare time this week. Last Sat. they had a crowd of potato pickers, and tomorrow they are coming again so that may finish it up. We still haven't had a frost, but the crops are looking scared.

The room was beginning to smell like roasted pork, and we took a break to stretch our legs and check on dinner. I was more aware of my grandfather's ticking clocks and how time here went unmarked except by these clocks. Sitting and listening to my grandfather talk, with the many silences that filled the spaces between his thoughts, time took on a different meaning. I didn't have to be anywhere but here, listening to his stories, and the intervening silences. If my marriage and inner life weren't so tangled, this would have been a simple existence.

In the kitchen, Henry started the coffee for after dinner. Filter in hand, he said, "After my mother was gone, you see, my Aunt Emma took care of me until my pop remarried."

I nodded, sipping spring water from a flowered glass. My grandparents had their own spring; the water was sweet like cherry wine. Betts got out plates and silverware.

"I remember one time, when I was two," Henry went on. "My stepmother was in the picture already, and she scolded me for something, and I cried. I was crying for my Aunt Emma, because I still thought Aunt Emma was my mother at the time. What should you expect of a child, two years old, who lives with a woman? He'd think she was his mother."

"That's true," I said. "There's a close bond at that age."

Henry looked down at the little throw carpet. "Emma was special. There was a special friendship there. She was more than just an aunt. But about my stepmother, I always say, she must have been a good woman. You imagine a girl stepping into a household with three growing boys. It must have taken a lot of patience on the part of that woman."

"And then she had her own children," I added, sensing his stepmother never considered Henry and his brothers her own.

"Two girls," Betts interjected, loading the pork chops on a plate with an oversized fork. The room smelled of browned butter.

"I try to look on the good side of things," Henry said. "There's enough evil in the world that a Christian has no business to take up. You just pick out the good things and repeat those, if you have to repeat something. But there is such a thing as keeping quiet and listening. You learn a lot more if you don't talk and just listen. If you're talking too much, then you're liable to say the wrong thing."

Betts whispered something to him that made him laugh. He returned to making the coffee.

I regretted bringing up his stepsisters. He'd wanted to say something else about his stepmother, and I'd pressed him toward a path he didn't want to pursue.

As we moved to sit down at their table, I asked about the true meaning of *schusslich*, a word I'd heard Betts use. I had a vague notion it meant "antsy," a word for restlessness my mother used. Henry and Betts went back and forth about the word meaning careless, or hurrying, until Betts concluded with authority, "It's a hurry-up thing."

Henry interjected, giggling softly himself, "There's one thing I'd like to ask somebody. How do they laugh in Pennsylvania Dutch? Do they laugh different than they do in English?"

Our laughter washed over the table while Betts put a platter of pork chops and a bowl of sauerkraut out, and we took our seats. Henry said the grace.

Typing up my notes later that evening, I wished I could be more like Henry, just laugh at what we perceive to be differences between ourselves as Mennonites and the world around us. But it wasn't my time yet to forget. This was my time to remember, and make my peace.

May 1, 1934. Yesterday we planted a truck patch. Planted Golden Bantam, Cassels, Golden Delicious, and White Evergreen sweet corn, yellow and green string beans, radish and cucumbers, also cabbage plants. I planted some speckled lima beans in the garden, also spinach, carrot, celery seed and Everlasting flowers.

Later that evening, I paged through the memoir of Henry's brother Norman that his daughter had compiled. I hoped to find more about Henry's relationship with his stepmother. I felt for sure that Henry was being too easy on her.

Norman told this story: two years after Henry's mother, Ella, passed away, Henry Sr. expressed interest in Ella's cousin Suzanna. Her father was displeased because he'd wanted Henry to marry his oldest daughter Mary. But of course Henry was in love with Suzanna, not Mary, so he followed his heart, and he and Suzanna were married. Suzanna's father happened to be a trustee of the Bally church, where Ella had been buried. This naturally meant that he oversaw the cemetery, and with this power, he got revenge on Henry. He saw to it that someone else was buried alongside Ella, making it impossible for Henry to ever be buried beside his first wife, as would have been the custom. When it came time for him to be buried, he was buried at Swamp Mennonite, where eventually Suzanna would join him.

When I read this, I understood better what Henry was saying. There was no point in criticizing Suzanna for her choices. There was enough of that while she was alive.

◆

Betts was taking on the role of interviewer. I was asking about Henry's childhood, but Henry was slow to answer my questions. Betts, a consummate conversationalist, was unable to bear the silence.

"You had to take care of your sisters, you said, while your mother, she used to work for a factory," she prompted him, leaning toward him in her chair. "She used to sew buttons. Why don't you tell that?"

"Well," Henry said slowly, "we sewed buttons. You see the pants always had—how many buttons?" He reviewed a pair of pants, pointing to the waistline of his trousers where the buttons would go: "One, two—three, four—five and six. Always six buttons for a pair of pants. Two were to button them closed, and at that time they wore suspenders, so they had two here in the front, and two in the back. I used to iron, too, I remember that. I had my own irons. They were lighter than the regular irons."

Betts urged, "Tell how you heated the irons."

"We heated them on a regular coal stove. We had three irons in a circle, and you put them back that way on the stove to reheat. Before school we did that. I'd get up at four in the morning."

"Four in the morning?" I repeated. "How old were you?"

"How old was I?" he asked, turning to Betts.

"You were ten, you said."

"Ten to age fourteen," he concluded. "And we had a chain pump for the wash and other things. A chain pump you turned the crank by hand, and the cups would come up through a pipe and bring your water up from wherever it happened to be—a cistern or a well. We had cistern water. Well, what is a cistern? It's when you save the water coming off the roof and store it in your basement."

Betts prompted him again. "Then you'd have to pump it into the wash boiler."

Henry continued, "You'd have to heat it on the stove in this wash boiler. And you'd have to tip it out of the wash boiler into the washing machine. Then you'd turn the washer by hand."

Betts' patience finally ended: "But you don't say it all," she scolded, sitting forward in her chair. "Then when you washed it long enough, you had to crank it through a ringer." She turned to me and asked, "Do you know what a water ringer was?"

Sept. 25, 1934. Summer is gone now, it seems I've been too busy to write. We sure had a hot summer. Everything in the garden and truck patch seemed to do well. We had all to eat we could. We sold a good bit and canned a lot, all my jars are full. I canned more this year than I ever did.

I shook my head, not sure what to do about the conversational morass.

"It's like two rubber rolls together," Betts explained. "You had to watch you didn't catch your fingers in the wringers."

"Then somebody else would hang it on the line," Henry added, swiveling in his chair a little. "I was too small to reach the line."

"That's a lot of work for a little boy," I commented.

Henry just nodded slightly.

I was about to call it a day—feeling bad Henry had to undergo that kind of drilling, but then Betts changed her tone.

"Why don't you tell the chewing gum story," she said, sitting back, seemingly satisfied by the extent of Henry's story. I noted out loud that if one person spoke at a time, then everyone would have a chance to speak. It felt odd to reprimand my own grandmother.

She looked at me apologetically, "Okay, now I'll be quiet."

"Okay," I said. "So what's the chewing gum story?"

"Down at Milford Square," Henry said, tapping his fingertips together, "that's where I lived as a boy, you see. We never had chewing gum, but we were curious about it. Then a man was working at our place once, and he was chewing on some. So we waited, and when he spit it out, my brother Norman fetched it. Norman chewed it. Then Nelson chewed it. And then I chewed it for a while. Just to see what it was like."

Betts slapped her thigh with a laugh at this old story, and I was glad for the break in the mood.

Chapter 2

Material

*M*y grandfather's humor always inspired me. It wasn't cutting like mine. My humor was like a chainsaw. And my life felt like it was sawn into so many pieces. I wondered if the pieces would ever come together—if I'd ever feel whole.

Guilt showered me with its blessings, like acid rain. I had left my husband, and in leaving New York, I'd dropped out of my Columbia University graduate program. I was full of failures. But that had become a project for me—tracking all my mistakes and missed opportunities. I had a mental list, like an inspirational calendar I visited nightly to feel terrible about myself. It started with watching "Planet of the Apes" as a child, and now this. Even though I no longer believed in God or that Jesus was going to return to separate the sheep from the goats, if there were such entities, I was definitely a goat.

One of the first things I learned in college was that I was the master of my body. I learned this completely drunk, slumped on the bathroom floor of some cabin at the end of a party. The ceiling was turning above me like a kaleidoscope, and one of my friends was puking in the toilet. She told me I should do the same. I was so offended as she showed me how she gagged herself with her middle finger. But I tried it. It worked. It worked great, in fact. Later, I used this technique to rid my body of anything I didn't want to keep—dessert, a bag of potato chips, my lunch. When my roommate started announcing her bulimic episodes, as in "I'm going to eat this whole piece of cake—and so what, I'm just going to throw it up," I was sure she was nuthouse material. At least I was discreet about it.

I love Picasso's paintings—his subjects' faces are like puzzles that don't fit together. That was how I felt about my life when I was twenty-six. I was broken apart to the degree that the pieces no longer made sense together. Although I'd gotten help for my eating disorder as a teenager, the ceiling of my life was still spinning. I didn't feel like the master of my body or my life at all. I was out of control, grasping for lifelines. In my dreams, I was always a boy of fourteen, pre-pubescent. I didn't know how to make choices about my future. How could I? It was chilling. All of my plans could be wiped out at any moment, and I'd either be nominated for hell—or be compost.

◆

Jonathan was going to Europe. His sister, Karen, called and said he was shopping for a backpack and tent, and he'd leave in just a few weeks.

"You're kidding," I interrupted. I had been pacing, but now I stood still, staring at the grassy hill outside my window, as if Jonathan would suddenly appear there with some explanation.

"How long is he going for? Where is he going?" I asked, trying to sound calm.

"He said something about a year," she said, aware now that this was the first I'd heard and wishing we'd stayed on the topic of my grandmother's cooking.

"Oh."

"He's talking about going to Europe and Africa, and maybe Asia."

"Asia?" I balked. That was three continents. That could take a lifetime.

"I didn't know you didn't know," she said.

I told her I was glad to know, rather than not know, and we said our good-byes.

I felt like an angry, fiery dragon—I wanted to hoard Jonathan away, even though I didn't know if I could love him myself.

I sank down into the sofa, and when I thought I wouldn't stop crying, I went to look in the bathroom mirror to wake myself up. That was me, I told myself. That girl with the red eyes and quivering chin. I was solid material—I had a self. If Jonathan never came back, I'd still have me. I washed my face, telling myself over and over again that that would be enough.

◆

When I was still living in New York, and Jonathan and I were throwing glasses against the wall in fights over the death of our marriage, our strong emotion seemed fake to me. We had never fought in the four years we'd known each other. We were peacemakers, according to our childhood faith and our family culture. His anger appeared to me like clown anger. A spoof of itself. I believed he was angry only because he knew he was supposed to be angry. I didn't think he really cared that I was leaving him. And if he did care, it was only because of what his family would think.

One morning when Jonathan was away, I opened a kitchen cabinet, took out all of our lunch plates, and set them on the kitchen counter. Rooting through the coat closet, I found the hammer Jonathan had given me for my birthday and brought it to the kitchen. I put one plate in front of me, raised the hammer, and cracked it into pieces. Shards of pottery flew back at my face and sailed into corners. I smashed the pieces, and when they were too small to smash, I put another plate in front of me. I smashed that one. And the next one.

The force of my body against the plates loosened something in my throat, and I began to scream at the walls. I yelled at Jonathan, because I didn't think he loved me. I yelled at my dad, because I didn't think he loved me either, and I screamed at my life, how completely screwy it had become. Hate and anger and rage came exploding like lava, like verbal vomit. When I had pulverized all eight plates, and my ears were full of the cracking sound of it, I sat down on the shards scattered on the kitchen floor and sobbed. I sat there until I felt like I had nothing left inside but emptiness.

If you were one of the Black-Eyed Susans watching me from the garden on the Hill, you would have thought my life a rather healthy one. Instead of drinking at the end of the day, I jogged up the Hill. Instead of smoking, I took walks in the woods and ate wild raspberries. I communed with baby raccoons, chased after toads, waded in streams. I was living in the womb of the world. Without a kitchen or restaurants to walk to, I ate most of my food raw—vegetables, fruit, nuts, yogurt. I ate little sugar, save for the pie Betts baked for her family on Friday nights.

But I was like an actor who has to cut her hair or gain twenty pounds for a part. I lived the way my family lived so I could fit into the culture I was recording. On the inside, I didn't look anything like them. A gaping hole stared me in the face now that I had no whiskey, junk food, or cigarettes to fill it with. It was a pit filled with pitch that threatened to swallow me up. It was my own living hell, a whirling black hole. It was the entity above me at the ceiling in New York that threatened to take me into it; it was the sinister face I saw in the woods. I raged against it, wanting to die but unwilling to take my own life.

◆

Melvin Miller, my therapist, was Mennonite, a fact that at first made him suspect. The last thing I needed was for someone to ask me if I had Jesus in my heart. But Melvin had degrees from Ivy League universities, and so I thought that put him on the outer edge of our culture. At the university, I told myself, he must have tasted the fruit of the world and felt the limits and the lures of his own culture thrown into relief. I took the number down from my mother, and I gave him a call.

Melvin was tall and thin and wore thick glasses that enlarged a pair of mischievous eyes that were also sponges, I felt, absorbing things about me in that first glance that I wasn't sure I wanted revealed. He looked like how I imagined Dr. Seuss looked, and his grin was just as animated. As we shook hands and sat down to talk in his small, paneled office, the sense I was getting from him was that he wasn't going to judge me. We were going to talk, and we were going to talk a lot.

Although the Amish have their *Rumspringa*, a period in which teenagers are encouraged to taste the world before joining the church, Mennonite rebellion is different. Everyone, even if you're a teenager, is supposed to avoid the leprous world. Temptations, we were told, go before a fall. As is the case for those who later take up membership in the Amish church, deviance from established rules can lead to two things. First of all, there's the process of reconciliation, in which apologies and change of behavior must be witnessed by the larger church. If that fails, there's the more drastic approach: excommunication. This is the fate right now of Mennonite gays and lesbians.

On the individual level, those excommunicated must relinquish their membership and benefits, some of them financial, such as mutual aid insurance. On larger level, this means entire local churches have been banished from the Mennonite denomination. I made the move first—I withdrew my own membership after college. Of course, the consequences of withdrawal are much less harsh in the Mennonite church than the Amish. I lost my cheap mutual aid health insurance, but I could still sit at the same table with my parents when I went home to visit.

Melvin wasn't surprised at the details of my own rebellion (which looked like a typical American teenage rebellion—sort of the point). Since he was a member of my parents' generation,

I was taken aback by his nonchalance. I guess I expected him to tell me where I went wrong and provide some Bible-based answers. Then I could have written him off and returned to my isolated, confused self. But that's not what happened.

He was so accepting, and I felt so validated, that I began to look forward to our visits like a child going to see Santa (not that I would know what it's like to be a child visiting Santa). But in each session, we would revisit the events of my life and see what compelled me to make certain choices; we would probe the internal logic behind it all. To Melvin, I wasn't crazy. I was a woman leaping internal and cultural barriers with as much force as I could muster. It was true that I had made some poor choices—like drinking a lot—but in seeing the internal logic of it, I was able to get a handle on making better, healthier choices. I was a woman who desperately wanted to love those around me, but I had to do some work first: I had to find a way to love myself. Melvin seemed so brilliant I began to call him my angel. Everyone, I came to believe, should have a Melvin.

After a couple of sessions, he suggested seeing Jonathan and me together. I was willing and, surprisingly, Jonathan wasn't opposed to seeing me. I wanted Jonathan to stick around, because I was afraid that if he left, he'd never come back. I didn't know if divorce was the answer for us. I was hoping that I could find some way to love him again. Jonathan, of course, having experienced my vast emptiness first hand, wanted to say goodbye, in as gentle a way as possible. It was humbling.

We made strained small talk in Melvin's dim-lit waiting room until the door opened, and Melvin called us in. We were like a pair of those roaches that ran across the kitchen counter of our New York apartment after a spray—their backsides all ruffled up, dying as they ran. I had chopped off nearly all of my hair, had smoker's breath, and wore the same blue cotton shirt I'd worn in college that now had a frayed hole on the sleeve. Jonathan had shaved his head completely at a time when it was popular only for Buddhist monks and Sinead O'Connor.

Melvin motioned for us to sit down, Jonathan on the sofa, me on the Lazy Boy chair. After some preliminaries, Melvin drew two dotted circles, overlapping slightly.

Jonathan and I leaned forward, watching this strange geometry.

"The dots represent a person who doesn't have a full identity," he said, looking at me.

I was crestfallen. I was sure he was wrong.

"When you don't have a strong identity," he said, "you rely on each other too much. You start finding fault with the other for not helping complete you more. But that's not a spouse's role. It's an impossible task for someone else to do."

"So what do we do?" I asked, wanting to swipe the paper away from him.

"Jonathan will go on his trip, and you and I will work on getting you an identity."

"What about him," I asked, as if Melvin was the parent, supposed to ground Jonathan in his room for bad behavior.

He faced Jonathan. "You said you want to go to Europe, no strings attached."

Jonathan nodded his bald head, and said flatly, "We've been through a lot, and I don't think it would work for either of us to be around each other right now."

I hated the lack of feeling in his voice, as if he were making an arrangement about the car. That, as I saw it, summed up our problem: he was in his own bubble, I obviously was in mine. Bubbles don't last forever, like marriage is supposed to. Bubbles float around until they burst.

"No strings attached, then," Melvin said.

"No strings," Jonathan shrugged.

They were both looking at me.

"Okay?" Melvin asked.

I wanted to shake them both. Don't you see? He's running away! I had thought that Melvin would try to keep us together, maybe tie up our claws or something, like lobsters.

"No strings," I replied, not looking at either of them, feeling as if someone else had used my voice. But I reached out my hand to Jonathan's extended hand, and we shook on it.

I imagined this over and over, meeting Jonathan at a restaurant. We'd be looking at the menu, going, "Well, so, what will it be—a Greek salad? Would you also like a divorce? Oh, sorry, you wanted the marriage? Okay, how would you like that done?" The worst part was not being able to look into a crystal ball and see, one year down the road, how he would answer. Not knowing, either, my answer. Feeling like I would crumble because I didn't even know what the answer should be. And the ultimate bad ending: what if we came up with different answers?

So while Jonathan would get a backpack and trudge off to Europe and Africa, I would spend Wednesday afternoons with Melvin. Those days Melvin would sit on his stuffed chair under the window, and I would try to sit still on the lazy boy, ignoring the voice in my head that told me to jump up and run away.

◆

A few weeks into our sessions, I began to bemoan how much time I had wasted looking for some kind of home in men or my work. I gave him a laundry list of mistakes.

He listened patiently as I talked, his legs crossed, his hands folded in his lap. After I was done, he said simply, "No time is ever wasted on the writer. For the writer, it is all material."

I snorted out a laugh.

"Material" was a word that sounded so clean and laundered, I could hardly relate to it. Material is what you worked on at a sewing machine, when you had your wits about you. My mom did that. She sewed pantsuits and dresses for my sister and me when we were kids. Material was something you could hold up in front of you and make sense of. See the stripes? You fit the pattern across the fabric so that when you sew the shirt, they don't look like they're falling.

Singing, gardening, and quilt-making are the traditional arts of Mennonites, the kind of art that is more communal than the kind of individual expression I employed through my writing. My grandmother's diaries are a good example of Mennonite expression. They are all about what she was doing on any given day for the community, or at least her family: gardening, washing, canning, church-going. No emotional goop there, just the stuff of everyday life, her very hard and stable life. It was difficult to think of my own floundering as having any lasting value, as being anything that I could learn from or use.

My childhood friend Patrick had asked me this question, the summer before I moved to the Hill: "Do you ever find yourself writing something instead of living it?"

We were sitting by a lake, listening to the geese. I had just read him a poem I had written.

"No," I snapped. How dare he? He didn't know anything about me or my life.

But sitting beside him on a picnic bench, I began to see that he had a point. Was I writing instead of living? Like the poet who throws down his pen and calls the person he was about to evoke on paper, I should have picked up the phone and called: "Hello, life, let's go do something." You know, skinny-dipping, or hang gliding.

"Sometimes," I explained, gathering my calm. "I have to write to live."

We were sitting facing a lake—a real lake and not a written one. I said that, and felt that I'd completely missed the point.

At the end of my session with Melvin, he sent me home with his copy of *The Prophet*, and told me to read the section, "On Love."

When I got back to my apartment, Clyde, my aunt's cat, followed me through the door. I sat down on the recliner, and Clyde performed his requisite stretches on my lap—his signal that he wanted a back massage. After this ritual, he snuggled in under my arm, stretched out along my thigh, and pretended to be asleep. I read the underlined parts first, about being shaken and ground down to smithereens, like flour, so that without your ego, you can be formed into something useful. You can be kneaded into bread for God's sacred feast.

My mother bakes loaves of bread that turn out so doughy you could use them for a pillow. That's how I want my life to be, I thought. I want to use the broken pieces of myself that are left to make something soft and edible and worth the time. My grandparents seemed to have turned out well, if pleasure is a good measure. My grandmother turned to the garden, quilts, baking, and conversation. For my grandfather, it was making electrical gadgets and fiddling with clocks. While some families may enjoy travel or playing sports, my family made things. This seemed to be the thing that brought us satisfaction. I wrote in my journal, "My family has been making patterns for generations. That is part of who I am. Patterns have the potential to comfort."

Before I moved to Pennsylvania, Patrick dragged me to a theater to see a corn-ball movie. He said I needed to laugh. My life had gotten horribly serious. At the time, when I wrote poetry, which I did almost nightly, it wasn't because I liked to dawdle around the music of language. I wrote because it alleviated the pressure in my head. But the notion of life as material introduced a different angle for me, an angle from which I could laugh out loud. I thought, sitting there with Gibran's book in my lap, that laughter was the thing that could dry out the pieces of my messy, puddly life.

Because it was zany, a crazy quilt. Here are some scraps from the torn fabric of my marriage:.

Triangle 1, puddle blue: Two Mennonites have shed all of their past except peace-keeping, a trait that they take too far, leading to a heavy, smoldering relationship.

Triangle 2, blood red: When the woman declares the relationship dead, the couple learns how to fight. They raise their voices, they break glass, they drop their emotional straight jackets and finally tell each other what they really think. But it's too late. She's moving downtown; he's planning his world tour.

Triangle 3 (part of corner missing), jet plane white: Seeing that he is leaving without her, the woman, not one to be left behind, begs him to stay. But he's made up his mind and thinks his wife is crazy, without even knowing about the bad faeries.

Rectangle 1, salt white: Not taken to looking back, the woman turns to look at the ruined city of her marriage. Like Lot's (offensively unnamed) wife, she turns into a pillar of salt. Or at least she cries that many salty tears.

Rectangle 2, clay: The girl, having previously discarded her heritage as irrelevant, steeps herself in it all the way like a mud spa.

Who ever said your life was going to be neatly packaged, like a UPS box, the doorbell ringing to tell you that you've arrived?

I stroked Clyde's back absentmindedly, until I noticed fur balls all over my lap. He was purring loudly, a deep cello sound. I stared at the high little window across the room. A gray light filtered down through the well. I wondered if Jonathan was up in the air yet. This was the day of his flight.

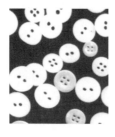

Chapter 3

The Minister's Daughter

I joined Betts in her fall ritual of collecting greens from the woods for windowsill terrariums. Betts and my Aunt June and I traipsed into the woods above my grandparents' house on the Hill. Meanwhile Henry amused himself with a newspaper in the car.

June was an only daughter who was born after five brothers and inherited not only Betts' button nose and eyes, but also her chutzpah. This meant that not only did she survive living with her brothers but outdid them in genius: while they hauled wood laboriously, she was cracking a book with one hand and vacuuming the floor with the other. June now lived in Bally, just below the Hill, with her husband Nelson and their own cadre of children and a few cats.

The air was chilly and moist among the spruce trees. Betts was keeping warm with a gauzy scarf on her head and tied under her chin, with Henry's red plaid flannel shirt buttoned over her dress. Our goal was miniature foliage—crow's foot, monkey tails, and wintergreen berries. These Betts would arrange with a landscaper's eye in glass terrariums and tend them as children, a bit of green to last the winter.

Betts and June pushed through the brown and yellow layer of leaves with sticks, unveiling a sprout of green here or there.

"Well," Betts exclaimed, disgusted. "There are a lot of leaves, but no berries!"

I was looking, too, though through the lens of a video camera I had borrowed. I zoomed in on her. She was bending over toward the floor of the woods with her thick stick, intent and focused. But I was new to video and not very discreet in my approach, if ever in fact there was a way to discreetly approach an elderly Mennonite woman in her forest ritual with the shark eye of a video camera. Betts looked up and saw me moving in on her.

"Oh, child! What are you doing? You're getting a little close!" she exclaimed, brushing back a wisp of hair that had escaped from her scarf.

I backed off, feeling ridiculous, apologizing for my amateur shooting techniques. It didn't belong here, this bulky technology. Their lives were simpler than that. They weren't self-referential at all—they were free from viewing themselves as sitcom characters, projecting images of themselves as they wanted to be seen. I had something to learn from this, and it had something to do with letting go of my cynical nature.

But that was just a vague idea I had, as I put the camera back in the car. Walking back into the woods, I picked up a thin branch, breaking off its twigs. It was time to look for berries.

◆

Later in the day, Betts sat in her customary stuffed chair, and at her feet, in a basket, were the beginning squares of a crocheted afghan for another of her grandchildren. This would make afghan number sixteen, for Jeremy, June's teenage son, the sixteenth grandchild. It was morning, and the sun was shining through the bay window. I commented on Betts' neatly arranged terrarium that sat on the sill, the rich greens and a smattering of the coveted red berries enhanced by the light.

Henry sat in his chair, his legs crossed, his long white socks showing. Betts put down her crocheting and began pulling out old photographs to pass to me. One was of her father, Pappy Kulp. He must have been in his late nineties for the picture. He looked frail in his wheel chair.

One was of Betts and her friends, posed with a bicycle for the camera. I asked her about the cape dress she was wearing.

"Oh, I wore a cape dress when I reached sixteen," Betts said, smoothing out her own dress, which was no longer caped. "Then I knew I had to, and I didn't like it. I always hated those cape dresses. But my mom said because Pop's a minister, and a minister ought to set the example, she would have to make me one."

She scrunched up her nose, which was a button nose that grew extra pink in the cold or with emotion. "I never liked it. I know just how it feels yet. It was a lavender material. My Aunt Mary had come and done sewing for my mother. And Aunt Mary bought some nice buttons to sew on this dress, and Pop wouldn't let her put them on. They were too fancy. She had to get some plain lavender. Ach, Mary didn't like this. Mary told Pop, 'They have to be a little different.' Pop said, 'No, those are too fancy.'

"But I wore such a dress for a long time. I guess it's twenty years since I quit wearing a cape dress. At that time a lot of my friends stopped wearing them, too. It was always an extra piece of material to sew."

Betts' dresses were now floral prints with high, scooped necks she got from her sister, Grace, who distributed second-hand clothes in Lancaster. She even went so far as to wear

Mar. 21, 1935. First day of spring. I baked shoe fly and raised cakes and boiled mush. Got some artichokes and canned them. Had our first dandelion[2].

brooches, though these were always of a subtle color and exhibiting a plant motif.

"Henry wore a plain coat, too, for a while," Betts continued. "But then they became so expensive to buy. A lot more than another suit. So he didn't wear it anymore. He bought others."

My father's own plain coat hangs in plastic in my parents' coat closet. After being mistaken for a priest in Levittown, it wasn't long before he switched to ties and leisure coats. My mother wore a head covering, but this she tempered with stylish clothes she sewed from Vogue patterns. As for my sister and me, maxi was chosen over mini, and aside from the hip pantsuits sewn by our mother, the hand-me-downs from cousins usually got to us post-trend.

"I was the daughter of a minister. You know how it is," Betts said. She waved her hand as if to say, "Don't ask more."

Since my father is a minister, too, I assume she meant the many church services, the way you were supposed to be perfect despite all the social pressures, the lack of money, the modest clothes. Is this what she meant? But she waved her hand. End of story. In collecting an oral history, you can be curious, but not nosey. If you are nosey, you may as well cap your pen and go home.

"We got by, as people do," she said. "My pop was an evangelist. He traveled out to Lancaster and held revival meetings for two weeks at a time. He must've preached at every church in Lancaster. He would come home Sunday mornings to preach at our church, in Bally, but then he'd be off again. He was a mail carrier, too, after he gave up farming. Those days, they didn't pay the preachers. And the preachers they chose by lot."

I asked Betts to elaborate because my memory of the details of choosing a preacher was a little vague.

Betts explained, "The men were named by the congregation, maybe three or four men. Then on a Sunday, they were asked to choose one of the Bibles that had been placed on the pulpit, see. One Bible would have hidden a slip of paper in it. Then the Spirit would lead the right man to choose the marked book."

"Now," Henry replied, clearing his throat. He'd been sitting quietly; I actually thought he'd drifted off. "If they really trusted the Spirit to choose, then they wouldn't nominate more than one man."

"That's true," I said, surprised at his criticism of the system.

"Well," Betts admitted, "some lots didn't work out so well."

Henry was once nominated for the lot, Betts noted in her diary. At the time, they still had six children at home. Accepting the lot would have meant that in addition to his regular twelve hour day job, he would also be expected to pay visits to the sick and needy, conduct funerals and weddings, and get fired up for a sermon on Sunday—none of it for pay, of course. Somewhere in there he'd find time to be a father. My mother's father, Ellis Mack, found himself in this situation: minister, farmer, husband, father of five, planting seeds and watering souls, in a period when people's salvation depended heavily on how they lived, a theology that held hands with the German work ethic.

Betts lifted the white, globed lamp from the shelf of the bay window. The window was a greenhouse of hanging ivies and potted cacti.

"This was my mother's coal oil light," Betts said. "Henry made it electric now. But mother'd put coal oil in it to burn. This is the lamp she'd take along up to bed with her. Not much light, not much to read by, like you do now."

April 19, 1935. I went along with Henry to Allentown. We stayed at Henry's parents' till he went over town on his route, then I did a little shopping. Got dress material for a weekday dress, 15 ¢ a yard. Also got some things for the children's Easter baskets. This eve. I made coconut candy eggs and dyed a doz. eggs for the children.

Betts placed the lamp back on the windowsill. "I wash that very carefully," she said in a quiet voice. "I'm always afraid it'll break." Henry was sleeping, head against the back of his chair.

"Are you listening?" Betts asked, loud enough to wake him.

Henry's eyes opened slowly. "Yeah," he said, voice crackling.

Satisfied, Betts continued, "My mother was a hard working woman. She had fifteen children. Eight died as infants. They had some kind of blood disease. I don't know that she ever whipped any of us. I really don't. She was a very hard worker. She had a large garden and did a lot of canning. She'd can a couple hundred jars of vegetables and fruit in the summertime. Yeah, she raised scads of berries, including three different kinds of raspberries.

"Mom always had a lot of company," Betts remembered. "When we lived in Lehigh County—that was before Pop was a minister—we came to Bally Church. We had twenty-five miles one way. We had a car by then. A '29 Baby Grand Chevy, it was called. We often brought people along home. It took an hour after church to get home, then you still had to make dinner. I often wondered—all of us girls wondered—how did she ever do all of this? I know every Saturday, she would bake a big dish of rice pudding and bake a cake."

The talk of food prompted Henry to go to the kitchen and return with a jar of peanuts, which he passed around. Betts asked if he could also bring the pretzels. Henry turned toward the kitchen, retrieving the tin.

"My mother wasn't so well," Betts continued. "She had heart problems when she was in her late forties. After that, she wasn't very strong. She would crochet but I don't think she did much quilting. She didn't have much of a garden. She had a little garden, but nothing like the big truck patch she used to have, where they had raised sweet corn and all that."

Betts paused and looked at the back of one hand, rubbing it as if to wipe away the age spots. "She died of cancer when she was sixty-nine," she said. "My sister, Grace, was working as a missionary in Honduras, under the Eastern Mennonite Board. She couldn't come to the funeral. They didn't have the money to fly home, and flying wasn't as easily done as it is now."

We started talking about missionaries, then, because Jonathan's parents had been missionaries to Somalia and Kenya.

"Well," Betts said, concluding our session. "We should have a little coffee to go with the cookies, not?"

◆

My great-grandmother noted the deaths of her young children in her diary. They were arranged by season.

Special dates concerning
the family of Elias W. and Elizabeth Rachel C. Kulp

Jan 25 1915 Elias C. Kulp died age 1 da [Asleep in Jesus]

March 2 1917 Ezra C. Kulp died age 9 mo 15 da [Fell asleep in Jesus]

March 15 1919 Daniel C Kulp died [Budded on earth to bloom in heaven]

May 4 1914 Hannah C Kulp died Age 8 mo 6 da [Gone to be with Jesus]

July 1922—3 Paul C. Kulp died age 10 da [So soon to be with Jesus]

Aug 25 1910 Samuel C Kulp died [Asleep in Jesus]

Dec. 5 1923 Miriam C Kulp died age 3 mo 12 da [Safe within the Fold]

Dec 11—1921 John C Kulp died [Will never know sorrow.]

◆

April 23, 1935. This eve. we drove up over the hills to see the peach blossoms. They are beautiful.

The extravagant bouquet of yellow leaves on the maple outside my door was now almost barren; the last few leaves hung on like shy children. Fall was my worst season. I could handle the brutality of winter, but not this gradual dying around me. Fall also brought the accompanying feeling that I should be doing something directional, but not knowing what that was.

Melvin was helping me see that a big part of my problem was a self-judge who was punching in too much overtime. Even leaving Jonathan was an event that I started to view less critically. I had used the metaphor of drowning to describe how I felt in New York; Melvin described my leaving as grabbing the closest, most obvious life-raft—the door. Whether it was the right or wrong life-raft was no longer relevant. What mattered now was what I would do with this life of mine that I had saved. Cheating the Grim Reaper by doing the job myself was a solution I no longer entertained.

If Jonathan and I had not been very good at marriage, we at least had started out as good companions. He was a third-culture kid—a child and grandchild of missionaries to Africa. Like me, he felt displaced in generic American culture and at the same time alienated from our own Mennonite tradition. For the five years we had known each other, we had served as each other's ally, holding onto each other while we drifted on the wide sea of the world.

In an attempt to keep the feeble thread that was left between us going, I'd written a few letters. But we had a no strings deal—we'd shook on it. Of course he wouldn't reply. He owed me absolutely nothing. It had been two months since my last letter, and nothing came in return.

Perhaps Jonathan would drop off the face of the earth, I thought. The mailman had come and left once again without delivering any airmail envelopes. The possibility gave me a chill that both made me shudder and feel somewhat lighter.

◆

Betts was excited. She'd been invited to talk at the mother-daughter banquet at church about the chores she did when she was a little girl. She'd prepared notes, and was now going to share them with me.

Up until now, I wasn't sure about her feelings about my project. Henry seemed to flow with whatever came his way. But I thought Betts might be wondering why I wasn't working so hard on my marriage. She did ask about Jonathan's where-abouts, but I could only give unsettling answers, like "in Europe somewhere" or "still traveling." I was glad that she felt engaged enough in the project to get excited.

Henry sat with us, paging through the newspaper, and I remarked that this was Bett's turn to talk again without interruption. As if that was a concern.

"At that time," Betts said, leaning forward, "we did extra house cleaning in the spring and fall. After the winter, you had coal dust; you had ash dust. And you had these heavy blankets in bed, and those made dust, too. We'd take the rag carpet out and hang it on the line. The men at noon, when they came in from the fields, they'd shake out these carpets, you know, shake the dust out of them.

"Then we had the weekly chores. We had six rocking chairs in the parlor. The parlor we used for company. We kept the door closed mostly to keep the dust out of it. And we had a sitting room to use during the week. My sister Mary and I had to wipe the dust from these rocking chairs, and you know they had a lot of fancy work on them.

May 1, 1935. This afternoon I planted the truck patch. I had two coats on and then I was cold yet. I planted corn three kinds, cucumber, squash, two kinds of beans, radish, gladioli bulbs, and all my peas.

"That's why I don't like old things," she said, shaking her head. "There's too much work keeping them clean."

The phone on the lamp stand rang, and Betts answered it. It was her niece, Miriam, who lived up the Hill. She was coming down to say hello. Miriam's house was next to the creek where as children we cousins prodded under rocks for crayfish. It was also next to the low bridge that went over the creek, where we crawled through, waving our arms to break the cobwebs, out to the other side. We always liked Miriam.

"Well, now," she remarked. "All these old stories. Have you heard enough now?"

She looked at Henry, out of habit.

"That's not for me to say," Henry answered.

I asked her to go on.

"Well, I'll say this yet. We always sat on the porch in the sun. Yeah, so every week on a Saturday we had to wash the porch. And it was my job to fill the coal oil lights and wash the globes because they often got smoked, you know."

Betts waved a hand. "Ach, then we had our knives and forks that had to be scoured. Every Saturday, you'd take wood ashes, and put coal oil on the wood ashes, then you'd rub them with a rag to take off the spots.

"Oh, you wouldn't know what it was like then," Betts continued, with a little laugh. I agreed. I didn't know if I even had chores as a child. I vaguely remembered cleaning out my guinea pig's cage.

"When I was about ten," she continued, "before my pop was ordained to the ministry, he wanted to have a bigger farm, so we moved to a one hundred and twenty-acre farm up near Allentown. That was away from all of our school friends. And we had to go to a different church." Betts paused, shaking her head. "And there we had a lot of work to do."

"When the men would be out in the hay field cutting the grain and all, my sister Mary and I had to take water out to the men. We had no ice cubes, no refrigerator to make cold water.

But we did have a cave down in the ground. I think there were eighteen steps down to this cave floor. And there we would keep the water so it would get real cold to take out to the men.

"That's right. We'd take peppermint water my mother had made. She'd put a drop of peppermint in and some sugar. Just a little more refreshing than plain water. We had a long ways to walk over a rough road. We had to hurry because the water would get warmer by the minute. We were glad if they had a rainy day.

"And one more thing," Betts said, slapping the armrest of her chair. "It was always my job to wash the outhouse, on a Saturday. You took a broom and a bucket and first you'd wash the seats, then you'd pour clean water on and sweep it off ,then sweep the floor. And you always had a Sears Roebuck book. You know how they say, 'Oh, oh, the Sears Roebuck book.' Well, that's where it'd be, if you'd need it: in the outhouse."

Betts forced a frown, and added, "That's why when some people say they'd like to go back to the 'Good Old Days'—no. I don't want to go back."

Miriam came, then, knocking and opening the door at the same time.

◆

Sunday dinner around Betts' table started with grace sung in four-part harmony, but the topic of conversation today veered off our usual topics of morning services, the day's news, and the weather. The usual crowd of Hill-dwellers had gathered: Uncle Roy and Aunt Sandi, Aunt June and Uncle Nelson, and their sinewy teen daughter Renee. We ate in the small din-

June 6, 1935. I baked 22 cakes for the route. I planted some more watermelon seeds The others came up very poor. I helped pick chickens this afternoon.

ing area that was wedged between the kitchen and the living room, enjoying one of Betts' Sunday feasts—baked ham, hand-mashed potatoes, and garden lima beans that she'd froze that summer.

My Uncle Roy was bantering with Betts about taking out a pesky backyard squirrel with a shotgun. I looked at Renee, perched on a while metal stool at the end of the table, and she was pushing her mashed potatoes around her plate with a fork. Roy is my father's twin, with the same salt-and-pepper beard, intense brown eyes and black hair. His build is a good one for a hunter: full chest, sturdy shoulders, held firm as if ready to let go an arrow.

Betts, who was known to behead snakes with a garden shovel, offered with teasing in her voice, "If you shoot that squirrel, I'll make him into a pie for ya."

The idea of taking a gun out back wasn't unprecedented. The summer before, after a Sunday meal, Betts had coaxed Roy to hunt a groundhog. The argument was that the beast had invaded her garden and eaten off a whole row of her peas.

"Sure—you dare do a good thing on a Sunday," she'd joked.

The squirrel's death sentence was sealed for bothering a bird feeder belonging to a couple of bird watchers, namely Uncle Roy and Aunt Sandi.

"How about it, would you eat squirrel pie if we made it?" Roy asked me from across the table with a wry grin.

He still liked ribbing me about the time I let out a scream after emerging from my apartment to find a gutted dear hung up in the garage.

But I was growing accustomed to this more earthy relationship with nature. After all, I grew up watching my grandfather Mack behead chickens in his barn, their wings flapping wildly after their heads were already in a pot.

"Sure," I said nonchalantly, trying to alter my reputation. "I'll try anything."

That night, we arranged ourselves around Aunt Sandi's table and ate gamy, peppery squirrel and potato pie. It was tasty, in an outdoorsy, save-the-birds kind of way.

♦

Starved for someplace to go, I drove Henry and Betts to Lancaster. We took the meandering back roads—100 South to 23 West—passing the neatly combed fields of Amish and Mennonite farms, and slowing down to pass the occasional horse-and-buggy. People have a hard time distinguishing between the Mennonites and Amish because many share some of the same customs. Some conservative Mennonite groups will wear conservative dress and use horse and buggy, making the distinction almost imperceptible from the outside. But a sure-fire way to tell the farms apart is to look for telephone and electrical wires. The Mennonite farms have them, the Amish ones don't.

After picking up sugar-free candies and shoo-fly pie molasses from Shady Maple, the equivalent of a Pennsylvania Dutch Mennonite Genuardi's, we went to dine at Bird-in-Hand Family restaurant. There you can eat five pounds of hearty Pennsylvania Dutch cooking for $5.99. It's a place where Mennonites and tourists mingle at the buffet and salad bar, and Pennsylvania Dutch is spoken at intermittent tables. The décor is very plain. And in the way that people in the Mennonite world are connected by very small degrees of separation, the proprietors of this restaurant are the older brothers of a high school friend of Jonathan's, a friend I also know from my days at Goshen College.

> May 20, 1935. Ascension and Memorial Day. I got up at 4:30 this morning and baked cakes. Today there was an all day Meeting at Bally Church. Topics were Have Ye Received the Holy Spirit Since Ye Believed, and The World and How the Christian Ought to Live in It. We were at Boyertown Church this eve.

At first, I thought my grandparents' gravitation toward Lancaster was for the good deals on pantry items, the lunches at Bird-in-Hand, or visiting Betts' sister, Grace, on the way home. But as I took these trips with them, I realized that what I was looking at was a whole community picture, where people like my grandparents lived and worked and played on a kind of historical stage.

In my grandparents' terrain near Allentown, Pennsylvania, there were a lot of Mennonites, but there weren't many Amish, if any. In Lancaster, however, for an entire day you could brush up against a community of people who were both your past and your present. Henry and Betts rode in horse and buggy as children, and wore plain clothes nearly identical to many we passed, strung up on outdoor wash lines like a stiff painting. For me, going to Lancaster was like looking into a time-warped mirror at the kind of life I would have led if I had been born a hundred years before. And yet, all of this history was still walking around, reminding you of how far you'd come from that place, and—if the spirit moved—how quickly you could return.

Car rides in my grandparents' Buick were always quiet, like riding a sailboat on a wide river. My grandparents rarely turned on the radio, and if they did, it wasn't to blast Madonna and sing at the top of their lungs. It was for news, or for the Pennsylvania Dutch talk radio. Now the radio was off. We looked out the windows at the silos and neatly combed fields as we passed, remarking about how the clouds looked like rain.

On the way home, we passed the bulk-food store where Betts like to buy her flour. I'd gone there once with her. After buying your soy milk and bulk sunflower seeds, you can pick up gospel tracts at the door, detailing how the reader still has a chance to save his or her soul from hell before Jesus returns.

"There are lots of different kinds of Mennonites and Amish, aren't there?" Betts asked from the passenger seat, breaking the silence. Henry was in back, his eyes closed.

I told her about my sister's elementary school teacher who once asked her where our mom parked the horse and buggy when she brought Juanita to school.

"Is that right?" Betts replied.

"Yeah."

"Well, I call them the buggy people," she said with a little chuckle.

For all of the talk about humility among the Mennonites and Amish, each group has its own sense of pride, whether it's Beachy Amish, Old Order Amish, Old Order Mennonite, or just plain old Mennonite. Humility, after all, is a pretty slippery notion. On a trip I took later to Lancaster, I went to an Amish-run health food store, feeling guilty as I shopped for being part of the big, wasteful world. The store was dimly lit with low gas lights, and perishables were jam-packed in generator-run refrigerators and freezers. I was comparing this to my own grocery store, where it was so bright and cold and electric that even in summer, I had to wear a sweatshirt to shop. I was falling into one of those dubious moods where I think of community life among the Amish as somehow superiorly simple, less anxious, more real. After all, they didn't concern themselves with keeping up with the Joneses, that flimsy set of wheels on which the American economy runs.

I was putting grocery bags in my car, when an Amish woman, all dressed in black, emerged from the door, and shattered my mood. As I turned on the ignition of my rust-laced Ford Festiva, I watched her strut across the parking lot to her well-groomed horse and shiny black buggy, tossing her wool shawl over her left shoulder like a New York diva.

4

Church Planting

*I*n the 1960s, my parents were planting a new church for Mennonites in Levittown, Pennsylvania. "Church planting" in this steel-mill town where there were only two Mennonite families, meant it was my dad's job as minister to first find people who were interested in Christianity, and second, get them to come to a Mennonite church. A few dedicated old time Mennonites came every Sunday as "anchors." They and my dad advertised; they knocked on doors. Of course, Mennonites being an unknown in our area, some people mistook my father in his black plain coat for a Catholic priest. Others guessed my father's accent to be Scottish.

Our meeting consisted of less than a dozen people and was held in our living room. So our house was our home, but also the "Levittown Mennonite Meetinghouse." There was a white wooden sign saying so on our front lawn. On Sunday mornings, already when I was two years old, I helped my sister put brick-red Mennonite Hymnals on each folding chair, and a neatly folded bulletin on top of that. Next, out came the lectern from where it was stored under the stairs. This arrangement worked well except on the Sundays when my mother had a roast in the oven for our Sunday dinner, and as the dark aroma filled the air, stomachs began to growl like a pack of bears. Between the aroma and the growling, I don't know how much people got out of the service.

After two years of living-room church my parents could cram in no more folding chairs so came up with another plan. An addition was built while we were conveniently out of town. When we returned, the door from our living room opened not to our garage but to the bright green rug and paneled walls of the new meetinghouse. It was odd, not because it was a church attached to our house—that was understood. It was odd because it didn't look like other Mennonite meetinghouses. Ours had folding chairs, not benches like my grandparents' church; the walls were paneled, not old celery-green-painted plaster; and there was my father's guitar up front, a really new thing.

It looked like a big living room. And in reality, it was a big living room. My parents were like family to a lot of people, listening to their problems, providing beds away from abusive husbands or exasperated landlords. Hitchhikers slept overnight on the meetinghouse floor, and teenagers sat in prayer circles there on Wednesday evenings.

Few of the women wore head coverings, and if they did so, they wore doilies, not the white mesh cap kind my mother wore and definitely not bonnets like my grandmother's. The men didn't wear coats—plain or otherwise—and almost everyone was young. The music we sang was different, too. We mostly sang Scripture songs written for guitar or pop love songs where the object of adoration was changed to God. While my grandparents and their fellow congregants crooned a cappella into their hymnals about the cross, we raised our faces and arms to the ceiling, as if reaching to touch the hem of God's skirt.

Sometimes, people even spoke in tongues.

◆

Going to visit my grandparents' house from Levittown as a child was like jetting to another country. Their house stood alone, on acres of land bordered by woods. Whereas at our meeting/house, parishioners were always stopping by or calling to bend my parents' sympathetic ears, in Bally we could go an entire day without the phone ringing. No one came by, either, with their bags in their car, hoping for a place to stay. The house was it's own entity, a place where people simply ate, slept, and looked for amusement.

The house on the Hill had a fantastic element, partly because of the woods but mostly because of Henry. Grandpop was an electrician, and so he was always fiddling with one gadget or another, finding a way to make his home life more economic, convenient, or silly.

I was concerned with the later, of course. I loved how he rigged the toy closet light so when you opened the door, the light went on and when you closed it the light went off. Each successive cousin spent time opening and shutting that door to try to catch—though never succeeding—the very moment the light went off. Then there was the pilot light outside the basement bathroom. If the room was occupied, a lit cherry-red pilot light on the wall by the door indicated that you had to wait. Above the light was a little wooden plaque that said, "Open in case of fire!" When you opened the flap, it said, "Not now, stupid, in case of fire!" I liked this numbskull humor. The only other plaque in our house had something to do with Jesus.

My grandfather's shop was in the deepest part of the basement, a place where he had manufactured the "Do-Nothing" box, a ham-radio sized box for his grandchildren to try out switches and lights and bells.

His workbench was scattered with wires and screws and other parts of some old appliance he was working on. The walls of his shop were covered with plaques.

It's too late to agree with me. . . . I've CHANGED my MIND! LOOK ALIVE! . . . you can be replaced by a button!

As a child lurching into my teen years, I stood at his elbow while he used pliers on a set of wires coming out like entrails from a radio. He was silent as he worked.

"What are you doing?" I asked.

Not looking up from his work, he said, "I'm trying to find out what's wrong."

I watched in the silence, transfixed by the mess of wires, the radio, the many tools with their sleek handles, the smell of basement cement.

One day Henry did a novel thing. He took the "Norelco" emblem from a discarded appliance and affixed it to the hood of his Volkswagen, where the ornament was missing. Then he repaired a rusting fender with strips of synthetic outdoor carpeting. My grandmother wasn't thrilled, to say the least, but it did save them money on repair. Then one day, my parents needed to borrow their car while ours was in the shop.

Everyone came out to pet the car after church. My one girlfriend asked delicately, pointing to the fake grass, "How come your grandpa put that grass on there?"

"I dunno," I said. "He just does stuff like that."

While my grandfather fiddled with the stuff of cars and appliances, my grandmother warmed the house with her pies and cookies by day, and her afghans and thick quilts by night. Grammie was one of those hub-of-the-wheel types, around which the rest of her family and friends spun. She was the local *People Magazine*.

"How is your friend, Ingrid," she asked, on a visit to her house. We were sitting in her living room, she in her chair and me on the green footstool, which was just my size and which was pulled up close to her. She bent forward, leaning an elbow on the chair's armrest.

"She's okay," I answered.

"And how are her parents?"

"Okay, I guess."

"Uh-huh." Grammie persisted. "How do you like school?"

"Okay. I like my teacher, but my homework is boring."

"It's boring!" she laughed. "Well, now why don't they teach you something interesting at school?"

"I don't know."

"Your daddy tells me you're taking clarinet lessons."

"Yeah, I play in the band. My band teacher is funny. He makes his own songs up for us to play."

"Well, now," she said, having finally obtained a tad bit more for her efforts. She'd cranked the engine, and now something was beginning to spurt forth. "What kind of music?"

"Just funny music."

"Oh, child," she said, laughing her cackling laugh and slapping her thigh.

This was the way she wrapped us all into her nest, grandmother hen amid a brood of grandchildren.

At night, my sister and my cousin, Tonya, and I stuffed ourselves into our sleeping bags on the living room floor, giggling to keep the monsters in the orchard across the street at bay. The night noises of this country house were torturous. I was used to the steady hum of traffic, the occasional revving motorcycle. But now the cricket chorus started to sing, and the clocks began to tick loudly like marching soldiers. Then the chiming would begin: first the coo-coo clock with its appearing and disappearing painted wooden bird, followed by the deep water sounds of the grandfather clock, and the tinny chime of the heirloom clock. No one thought to turn the clocks off for the night so that we could sleep. They were like pets—they were part of the family.

Despite the monsters and the clocks, if it had been my choice, I'd have stayed on the Hill and let the parishioners for someone else to save. But at the end of our stay, we lugged ourselves back to our Levittown Mennonite Meetinghouse, so we could fold bulletins, hot off the mimeograph machine, for Sunday worship.

♦

When I was thirteen, my family moved to Doylestown, Pennsylvania, and I went from a prefab Mennonite world to the historic Christopher Dock Mennonite High School world, my mother's alma mater. In Levittown, I'd hung out with girls who liked playing Battleship while listening to Led Zeppelin. Here the popular thing to do was to go to friends' houses and have Bible studies. But I felt elated when I was invited to one because it was being hosted by one of the popular girls. We filled her parents' overstuffed living room with our teenage heat; I sat with others on the floor. There were about twelve of us, or some other biblical number. It was all very serious. We read the Bible. We prayed. Although this was the language I knew, it was not the culture I knew. The most exciting thing that happened was that a cute, popular guy named Mark prayed out loud. I felt I'd woken up on Pluto. I was different all over again.

Although as an adult I followed my own brick road and avoided religion, I still puzzled over the question of what I could do to be like Jesus Christ and how I would live if I gave away all of my possessions. It wasn't a religious question, but a social justice one. I felt certain I should be an Abbie Hoffman or a Mother Theresa, but I just couldn't see myself being very effective with people like David, the man who hung around our New York block and wore plastic garbage bags on hot August days, or the older man by Columbia University who followed students around with his toothbrush, begging for money for a tube of Crest. My last job of teaching elementary students in an impoverished neighborhood on the Lower East Side was a failure because I saw each child as my responsibility to save, and I couldn't even teach them to speak English well. My high expectations coupled with mismatched skills were major hurdles, giving me a clear sense that I'd make a really bad Jesus Christ.

But that didn't mean I didn't wrack my brain trying to think of other ways of being Jesus Christ. Between inheriting a German work ethic, along with the Mennonite view of the world ("Sin-sick" was how my grandfather Mack referred to it), and growing up as the offspring of mission workers in the age of holy rollers, I felt changing the world was my responsibility. On the Hill in Pennsylvania, however, something occurred to me one late night, when I was lying in bed and troubling over whether journalism satisfactorily contributed enough to people's lives. I decided that I had a too-narrow definition of valuable work. Wasn't I working? I was writing an oral history. Furthermore, I was keeping an elderly retired couple company. I decided that this was work enough.

In my work ethic book, the arts do not appear anywhere. My plan appeared under the "selfish" heading and was cross-referenced under "leech." But I decided to close that book and put it on a shelf, where hopefully it would be eaten by worms and pooped out as psychic compost. I sat down and figured out how many freelance articles I could write to meet the rent and pay for peanut butter, crackers, and car insurance. It wasn't much. It made me feel light, like a paper airplane.

The following morning, I sprinted up the Hill and back, thrilled with my plan.

When I came back, sweated and happy, I tore out some airmail paper from my desk drawer and plopped down on my sofa to write another letter to Jonathan. I told him about what my grandfather had said about doubting his life, about the log in the woods, and my decision to call my creative writing my sole work and live off the ether. I wanted him to know that I was getting some glimmers of hope apart from him. This, I wrote, didn't mean I didn't have any love for him. It simply meant that I was changing my assumption that I'd be forever depressed, like one of those pieces of garbage that gets stuck on the bottom of a dumpster and stays there forever. I was beginning to peel myself off.

5

How Did We Get Along?

*T*he wind was forcing the clouds on a rampage southward. It looked like a storm brewing. That was it for the leaves. They were all coming down now.

We were sitting in the living room again, Betts in her chair, crocheting on her lap. She was making a block afghan, like the multicolored one on the back of the davenport.

I'd warned Henry and Betts a few days before that I wanted to talk about their dating days and early marriage, but after I asked about their first date, we sat in an uncomfortable silence.

Betts chuckled, embarrassed. "Well, I don't know."

"Well," Henry said, scratching his chin.

Finally, Betts launched in.

"Well, every time I'd see Henry," she said, "I thought, boy, he's a nice fellow. But he was dating this other girl, Ella, you know. And I was dating that Huber fellow. I dated him pretty long, but I just never cared for him. I guess I just dated him so I could get away, is that how it was?" She was leaning forward in her chair, her ankles crossed.

"I don't know," Henry conceded.

"Now I wasn't forward—I didn't go after him," Betts continued, "but after Henry's girlfriend died, I quit that Huber fellow. I thought I might have a chance."

Here, Betts paused—her face lit up. She brought a hand to her chest, as if she surprised herself. "Now don't write that down! I didn't tell that to anybody! I didn't even tell you, Henry, did I?"

Henry was grinning. His grin was always a half-smile that reminded me of the Buddha.

"I guess you suspected it," Betts said, egging him to respond.

"No," he said, with a pause. "I didn't know that."

I asked Henry to talk about their first date.

"Did you ask her on a date?"

His voice was quiet. "I remember when church was over, in back where the cars are parked," he said. "We'd walk back there and the fellows would say which girl he'd take home. So someone said, 'Well, how is Elizabeth going to get home?' I said, '*I'll* take her home.' I asked her if I could drive her to Allentown. I guess that's the first date we had."

"All of us girls," Betts added, "we would stand on the porch to wait for the fellas, and we'd all watch and we'd see who fetched who. I was always glad to tell the girls who I had gone with."

Henry said, "I guess there was a couple of weeks I didn't come to see her, after that first drive home."

"Yeah," Betts replied, accusingly, "then I was afraid he wouldn't come anymore."

Henry teased, "She didn't write and tell me to come."

"Well," Betts said, waving her hand, "they didn't do it that way. If a girl would've asked to drive a fellow home in those days, why, oh! That would've been the worst thing. If I'd have asked you, you wouldn't want anything to do with me, then, would you, Henry?"

"No," Henry agreed, "that wasn't the way they did it those days."

♦

There's this feeling, when you're around family whose lives have worked out okay, that you should hide the details about your own scrambled eggs of a life. I didn't talk to anyone about the extent of my depression, not even Melvin. I told different people different bits of it, but no one got the whole McCoy—the weird faces, the blob above my bed, my urge to jump in front of a train, the way I punished myself for not being the generous, loving, world-saving Christ figure I knew I should be.

I was afraid if people knew the extent of what was going on in my head, they would lock me up with the other lunatics. That's what they'd done with my two friends at Mt. Sinai. The white walls, the white beds, the locked corridor. The experimental drug cocktails, the floor mates who thought they were Jesus or that you were their mother—I was sure such a place would make me comatose. At least on the Hill—with people who were so sane they should sign up as sanity's poster children—I was master of my own roomkey.

Betts began talking about their teenage years when Henry's first girlfriend, Ella, died of typhoid. I asked Henry how that affected him.

"Hm?" He asked, adjusting his hearing aid. I repeated the question. "The school house well was contaminated, and a lot of the people carried that disease."

"Typhoid fever," Betts prompted.

"Typhoid fever. That spread. Then did Stella get that?"

July 9, 1935. Heavy rain all night and this morning. It just poured down for quite a while. Very high water. The flood records were broken for this section. Many bridges washed away and roads impassable. Also bungalows were washed away along the Perkiomen. . . . Many chickens drowned where chicken houses were washed away. This eve. we went up home to pick some raspberries to can. They spoiled pretty much in the rain.

(Henry's brother, Norman, was dating Ella's twin sister, Stella.)

"No, she didn't get it," Betts answered.

Henry explained, "We met these girls at church, Norm and I, and they were only what, fourteen. We didn't know how old they were. And their parents said, well we weren't allowed to date children, not until the girls turned sixteen. We didn't date for two years," he said.

"Then you dated her long," Betts said. "She was eighteen when she died."

"What did you do? That must have been devastating," I asked, still wondering how this affected him.

"There wasn't much to do," Henry said. "We buried her."

Memory after sixty years, I reminded myself, is selective. What a person tells about those memories is highly selective. I was frustrated; I wanted details. But there it was: it happened, it can't be changed. It was just like Betts' diaries. Everything is matter of fact. I, on the other hand, am a product of psycho-analysis culture. I'd like to know how it all feels. But this is not their culture. Their culture is *God's will.*

"Norman and Stella married soon after this," Betts said.

The cuckoo-clock chimed, followed by the other clocks.

"When I worked on the farm, the Hubers. . . . " Henry stopped, looking at me. "Now don't write this down."

"Or we won't tell you," Betts said, wagging a finger and laughing.

I agreed, putting down my pen. But I didn't turn off the tape recorder, and no one noticed.

Henry started again, "When I worked on the Huber farm as a boy, they had a son about my age, and he used to date Betts before I knew her."

"Well," Betts corrected, in a scolding tone, "that was after you weren't living there anymore."

Henry nodded, nonchalantly, and continued. "Norman and I talked about her, and we knew she was going with her parents to a certain church—Providence Church—so we went there. He said he was going to ask her for a date, and I said I was going to ask her for a date, and I said, *The best man wins*," Henry chuckled.

So this is the story I couldn't write down—no Mennonite wants to be caught saying he's the best man. Humility is valued over self-assertion. But there it was: Betts went with Henry, and not the Huber boy.

Betts retrieved a photo album from her lamp stand, its black-and-white photos fastened with corners to brittle black paper. Betts came over with it to sit with me on the davenport, leafing through the relic, telling me which of the friends had died, and from what causes.

"Fifteen or more of us young people used to get together," Betts said, turning the pages carefully, resetting photos that slid out. "We always thought we had good times. Out at the Longacre farm, they used to flood their meadow in the winter, you know, and that was such good skating. The meadow would stay frozen all winter. We just had colder winters than we do now."

As she was talking, I was thinking about global warming. I knew the frog population on the Hill, like in many areas, had diminished. But I found my perspectives to be gloomy, where even my grandfather's occasional grumblings about getting old were ameliorated by his belief in mansions in the sky. I imagined that their faith made them adaptable to the ravages of life.

"A gang of us," Betts continued, "used to go up the mountains. I have to show you some of those pictures. Some of those old Fords." She paged through until she found the picture she was looking for. There are a bunch of kids, dressed in dark clothing, standing in front of two 1920s Fords.

Aug.16, 1935. I dried a big drier of corn, canned tomatoes, string beans and pickles, also put 75 pickles in a crock for sweet pickles.

"Look," she said, amused. "There they tried to stand on their heads."

"For our wedding," Betts said, "Mom made a chicken dinner. That was the second of October, 1927. Uncle J.C. Clemens married us. I still remember the song "Lord Be Our Wedding Guest" and Uncle David Allebach playing the organ for it—such a pump organ. Then Monday we moved to Allentown."

Henry added, "That's right. I bought the house that my pop had lived in on Hall Street, 743 South Hall. We took the day off to move."

Betts got up to walk to the kitchen, which was separated from the living room by an island. "In those days, after a wedding, friends would come around making such a noise. They called it a Bull Band or a Dutch Band." She rooted through a drawer, returning with a silver spoon full of nicks and dings.

"They banged kettles with spoons," Henry explained. "Then you brought the folks in to treat them."

Betts added, "We gave everyone soda and pretzels, most likely—that's all we had, then!" She pointed to the spoon, "That they left as one of the presents. I still use it to measure my lard for pies." She corrected herself, "Or Crisco is what I use now."

"I worked in a stocking factory then," she continued, "and they gave us silverware."

"You worked in a factory?" I'd always pictured her doing chores on the farm or in the house. A factory was a more secular place.

"A lot of my friends worked in factories before they were married," she explained. "I used to like to go. We had a lot of work at home—we raised berries. But when you worked in a factory, you could get away."

I, too, worked in a factory, for six months after high school, when I was trying to decide what to do with myself. Sticking my head into a hot oven in August to bake orange computer screens whose function I didn't even understand hastened my decision to go to college. But Betts must have liked something about mending socks. Even after she left the factory, she kept mending them—this time for the homeless. Even at eighty-something, she received big boxes of socks from that same factory, to sew, pair, and send to the Bowery Mission in Manhattan. I'd seen these boxes of socks for so long—put out at Christmas for family to select our own favorite pairs—that when I happened by the Bowery Mission on my way to Chinatown one fine New York day, I felt like I'd walked onto a page of a fairy tale.

I asked Betts what I thought was a fairly obvious question: "Did you ever feel different as a Mennonite?"

"No, you daresn't think that way," she said, her voice sharp.

"Oh," I replied. I felt rebuffed. I hastily changed the subject, and we concluded our conversation for the day.

That evening, I tried organizing my notes while Clyde lounged on the stuffed chair. My grandmother's terse response had surprised me. Maybe she misunderstood, I thought. Maybe she assumed I meant superior, which would of course be an obnoxious question. What I actually meant was the exact opposite—if she'd felt apart from her peers, somehow less than. This, after all, had been my experience. I felt that others could attain things that I couldn't. And not only material things. Ephemeral things that had to do with the world, like worshipping the BeeGees, for instance.

I didn't bring it up again with Betts. I decided, given my own conflicting notions about my tradition, that if someone had asked me the same question, I might get snippy too.

Oct. 27, 1935. We were at Swamp Church. Well I think we felt better when we went than we did when we came home, as they read the names of those that are in the lot for minister. Only two have been voted for. Abe Yoder and Henry. The Lord only knows which one will be chosen.

◆

"How did you two manage together for all these years?" I asked, sitting in their sunny living room. This year, they'd be celebrating their sixty-fifth wedding anniversary. I hadn't made it to three. My question was followed by silence, as usual.

I was becoming somewhat used to silence. Silence after I asked a question, silence from Jonathan, silence from my basement apartment walls. I was learning to wait through it . . . taking a deep breath, blowing out through my nostrils the smoke of my anger and impatience.

Betts protested, "Other people can sit down and rattle things off. I can't do that."

"Well, you're usually pretty good at talking," I said.

She laughed. "You live one day at a time, that you do."

I nodded. In the silence that followed, Betts inspected the sunspots on the back of her hand. I doubt if she'd ever used sunscreen in all of her gardening hours. Instead she wore a white sunbonnet with a ruffled edge, striking the kind of image, out there in her bean patches, which collectible dolls are based on.

"One thing," Henry said casually, with a little pause. "You don't die before the anniversary."

"Oh, Daddy," Betts laughed.

I wondered if my husband's persistent absence bothered them. They occasionally asked where he was, but not why he was there. My mother told me that Betts had asked her, but my mother deferred any response to me. Betts didn't ask me. She probably knew better.

What could I have said? None of my life as I'd lived it would make any sense to them. A vow is a vow is a vow, in their book. For all of their adaptation to the world around them, they did not cut themselves on its rough edges. They were part of a Mennonite community where their Christian values were a constant, and a split marriage was a scandal. In their tradition, worries and cares were bathed by the balms of Gilead—their faith and community.

"If you believe in God and trust him," Betts said, cutting into my thoughts "he will help you through. Have God first in your life and in your home."

I nodded, blandly. I had no idea what this meant. The words were familiar, but I had lost track of what it meant to have "God first." When I was a kid, it had meant going to church, putting part of my allowance in the offering, and saying prayers. When I grew up, I stopped believing in God. I saw God as a deity who required that I earn his approval. Always failing, I wearied of trying. In what Betts said I tried replacing God with "goodness," but that seemed a thin stew.

I asked my grandparents if they could give me specifics, but they deferred to their sons—Henry Paul, Roy, and my dad—who were ministers.

"Having the same high ideals," Henry explained. "Believing in God, and in his son, Jesus."

"That helps you through some hard times," Betts said, rubbing her hand again.

Ah—shared ideals. This was a problem for us. Our ideals had to do with social justice, and since both Jonathan and I had been working with poor populations in poorly funded public schools in one of the world's most powerful cities, we'd developed a certain cynicism around those ideals.

Henry added, "It does take a lot of patience. If one person is right, he isn't right all the time. There isn't such a thing. I call it give and take."

"I believe in talking things out," Betts answered, "not harboring things in. That isn't right. Oh, Daddy," she continued, waving a hand, "you always have a lot of patience. I'm different. I want things to go quick."

Oct. 31, 1935. Well, today was this ordination at Swamp and Abram Yoder was chosen by lot to be our new minister at Swamp. That left us free.

I nodded, recognizing myself in this.

Henry shook his head in generous disagreement.

"Yeah, you agree that I'm more impatient."

Henry started to say something, but then a fire siren started blaring, and Henry wondered out loud what it was.

Betts told him, and that led to talking about getting him a new hearing aid before Thanksgiving.

"I still think I'll make a pig stomach," Betts added, free-associating. She asked me if I'd ever eaten pig stomach.

"Oh yes, plenty of times," I replied, surprised that she would have forgotten this. "Last Thanksgiving it was in Roy's basement."

That was before it was made into an apartment.

"Two years ago," she corrected.

"That was when Jonathan tasted it for the first time," I said. "That was the test to see if he could be part of the family."

"And he liked it, didn't he?" Betts asked.

"He liked it."

"I don't know any in our family that don't like it. They don't all like the skin. But I know your cousins, Tonya and Dione, they used to almost fight for it!"

Pig stomach is a dish always served with some ribbing in our family. Betts always called it by it's real name, not the more formal "Dutch Goose." The dish, while it sounds distasteful, is actually a tasty mix of pork and potatoes, and lots of black pepper, boiled inside (and this is the unsavory part, so you try not to think about it too much) the membrane of a pig's stomach.

Betts added, "I know the way the skin is good—I fry it the next day, you know, with the other ingredients."

I looked forward to this feast. It fit the picture of my life at that moment: how unsavory it appeared from the outside, and how good it turned out to be for my soul.

Betts noted that the fire siren was still going, which circled us back to where we were before: relationships.

"What were we saying?" I tried to prompt.

Betts looked at me pointedly, "You don't run away from it when something goes wrong." I nodded, poker-faced.

She continued, with a stern look, "And there will be times. You work on it until it feels right."

I scribbled notes. I wondered if this was for me. Or if she was remembering times she'd wanted to run away. I took her lesson like a lesson she'd given me once on making pie dough. You add water to the dough "until it feels right." After sixty years of doing it, she knew what "right" was, both for dough and marriage. But I didn't have her patience with my marriage. I saw a deep, swallowing hole, and bolted.

Betts continued, "I know one thing, in the Thirties and up until twenty years after that, a lot of churches would have Bible instruction meetings, and the churches were full. They'd have to carry in chairs."

Henry added, "I think with education and money, people can help themselves. They don't have to depend on God."

In their culture, depending on God was part of living in a community. There was a shared theology, and a shared set of rules and traditions based on that theology. Staying with one's spouse was one such rule. In the culture I had surrounded myself with—a loose amalgam of people like myself who wanted to be all new—rules were as clear as the Hudson River.

Henry paused, then continued, "But you see, they'll say, 'He's just a dumb Dutchman.'"

I snorted out a laugh. Dumb Dutchman sounded like one of Henry's little witty compositions. Then I realized my error.

"What?" I asked.

"Well," Betts said, "coming out with things like this. People will laugh at us. You don't have to show this to anybody."

Jan. 22, 1936. I went over in the woods this morning and got four baskets of sticks together again before it rained so fast. I did my mending and cut some stockings for a rug.

I was appalled. Of course I would show this to somebody. I wasn't recording these stories for wallpaper—though that's an interesting idea. I told them they were wise, that their experiences were valuable to me. The fact that they made the best of it together for sixty-five whole years said something about them.

"You'd be hard-pressed to find that kind of commitment among people of my generation," I argued. Then I stopped. Maybe that had meaning to them. But I also realized something that hadn't occurred to me before. They probably had visits, too, by that tired old judge who sits on your shoulder and tells you negative things about yourself. He says horrible, untrue things such as, "You're nothing special," or "You're not good enough," or "Who are you kidding?" This judge came to visit me quite often. A control freak at his superego heart, he was never pleased by acts of self-assertion.

"That's the way I look at it," Henry said, tapping the tips of his fingers together. "You see, people think I have no education. Well, I don't. As far as schooling is concerned, I never made it through eighth grade. Then I had to stay home and help with the farm. At that time, I was a hired boy, and the boss needed my help. I don't have any, I guess you call it, formal education."

"Well, Daddy, you got a lot more than education—you got a lot of experience," Betts chided him.

"Sometimes experience is worth *more* than education," I chimed in, but I knew about judges. They chatter loudly—they pretend they're the only voices in town.

"Isn't it nice today?" Betts said with gusto, graciously moving us away from Henry's self-flagellation.

"Gorgeous," I responded. It was one of those days not too hot, not too cold, with a light breeze that cleansed your skin.

"You didn't sit down in your basement the whole day, did you?" she asked.

"No, I walked back from Bally. I had to go down to make some copies, and I walked."

"Good," she said.

I went back to my room with my notes.

Dumb Dutchman. This was what I was trying to get at when I asked my grandmother about feeling different as a Mennonite: the sense that people from the outside might not understand you. That you might be ostracized for not being fully American, whatever that is. Didn't people still throw rocks at Amish buggies? Why was I so shocked that someone called my grandfather a Dumb Dutchman? There were so many names to call people different from yourself.

Yet being a Dutchman wasn't necessarily connected with being Mennonite. On the Hill in Pennsylvania, most people were "Dutch," the term derived from *Deutsch* (German). So not only was he different from the world as a member of a Mennonite enclave, but he was also someone who grew up in a Pennsylvania German-speaking community in an English-speaking world. (This is why people of the world are called "The English" by the Amish.)

Language itself was a barrier. For the Amish, the barriers serve a purpose. For the Mennonites of my grandparents' generation, who wanted separation from the world but also believed in sharing their faith, their language was simply an outcome of living in a certain region of America. When the pressure came to learn English, they did not resist.

Maybe it helped that I was there, on the Hill, in my next generation, ever-so-slightly modern shoes, to celebrate my grandparents' difference from the world. Betts laughed when she first saw my actual shoes: narrow, laced black boots that reminded her of the kind she hated to wear as a child. But I imagine she liked my shoes, how this somber style had been resurrected into something playful—and worldly.

Jan. 23, 1936. It keeps me almost busy to keep enough fuel here for the fires. This eve. we picked chickens in the barn and got awful cold.

6

Ingrid,
Anthony,
and Annamarie

*I*t was 1970-something, and my family and my best friend Ingrid's family were taking a hike along a path in my grandparents' woods. Ingrid and I were up front, poking our walking sticks into the bushes. We were eight, friends since age two. The bonding of children and our parents' friendship stuck us together like grafted trees. Her parents were Indonesian and Dutch—actual Dutch, not Deutsch, and her father's Dutchy accent endeared him to me—it echoed in my ears like my grandparents' way of shaping words.

Ingrid always said I was the lucky one because I got the wooden spoon, and only once in a while. We didn't even get whipped after my sister and I hid all of the spoons in the house, she pointed out. I told Ingrid she was lucky because, even though she got the belt on a regular basis, at least she could wear halter tops that let her navel show and listen to rock and roll on her radio. She could watch cartoons and even *Planet of the Apes*. She could wear pants to church on Sunday morning because *she* was not a preacher's kid.

On our walk, we were in a wooded world that belonged only to us. Our parents' attention was on each other, our sisters walking together back there somewhere, too, and so we could pretend we were lone explorers in this tangled nest of woods. The air smelled of wet leaves and bark, though the woods were dry. I kept an eye out for toads and toadstools.

Then everything changed. Ingrid shrieked, and her father swung his shoe at her head. Everyone was shouting, and I felt stings on my head. I took off after Ingrid, thrashing through the woods, jumping over roots and fallen branches, out onto the road. Her father chased after her, waving his shoe. My feet pounded hard on the pavement, bolting down the hill, letting gravity pull me forward toward my grandparents' house.

As I passed her father, I remembered the time in their back-yard when he'd chased Ingrid around the cherry tree with his shoe, until she and I both ended up in their upstairs bathroom, sobbing, under her mother's hovering presence. The memory made me run faster. Around the bend was my grandparents' house, and we bolted inside, one after the other. Grammie howled as yellow jackets trailed us in. She went after the remaining swarm with a towel and fly swatter.

We sat in the pink-tiled bathroom with its scent of rose-perfumed soaps, with our mothers inspecting our heads, and Ingrid and I sobbing and heaving for breath. Ingrid was sitting on the toilet, and I was on the edge of the tub. Our mothers swabbed our wounds with ointment, comforting us in gentle voices. Evidently one of us had stepped on a yellow jacket nest, which is why they had swarmed us. Somewhere in their exchange, one of them mentioned the word *poison*.

Ingrid burst out, "AM I GOING TO DIE?"

It struck me funny, for some reason—dying from yellow jackets? My sobs turned to a sudden laugh, a loud, half-sob laugh dulled by the small, tiled room.

"Stop it," Ingrid said shooting me the squinted-eye look we had practiced perfecting on each other.

I stopped, wiping my laugh away with the back of my hand, and looking down.

"No," her mom reassured her. "You won't die."

Our mothers announced the tally—Ingrid had fifteen stings and I had only eight. Ingrid looked triumphant. I gave her the best "I don't care" look I could muster.

Then Ingrid was wrapped in an afghan like a cocoon on the sofa. I wanted her to get up and play with the marble roller, but she was worn out, and I felt sorry for her head, all stung up like that, and swatted with a shoe besides.

Spilling out of Grammie's afghan, Ingrid's black shining hair covered any evidence of the stings. My own stings ached dully. Our parents were in the kitchen having coffee and one of my grandmother's summer pies. I ate cookies on the floor.

The image of her father running after us with a shoe kept repeating itself in my mind, until I began playing with the marble roller, and the clunking sounds drowned it out.

Walking through these woods as an adult, I wanted to see Ingrid again, now that we were our own people, and shoes and spoons were far behind. I tracked down her phone number through my parents, and called her up one night.

"Hey, girl, how are ya?" she practically yelled, and her Philadelphia accent was still there, drawn out from her new home town, Philadelphia, Tennessee.

I brought her up to date on my recent life I wished that I had something more successful to tell her—something that would wow her and make her glad to talk to me. But as I talked, I realized that's not why friends call up old friends. She brought me up to speed on her life, too: her own marriage, four children, and a pot-belly pig.

"I didn't think I'd ever hear from you," she said. "Last time I called you, you seemed like you didn't want to talk to me."

I fished around for an explanation. She was right. I was in college and thoroughly confused by my childhood, a time I associated with a naiveté, a state of mind I didn't want to recall.

The same year I had received another call, this time from our mutual friend Anthony. Anthony was a little older than Ingrid and me, my sister's age. At Levittown Mennonite Meetinghouse, he was the son of an Italian barber who put Christian words to popular songs and taught them to the congregation. Anthony and his sister Annamarie were friends I admired from a distance. They seemed to embody the physical and mental stature that I knew I would someday have, when I was bigger. Since their mother smoked, they also had the worldly allure that many of my friends had, which I promised myself would be mine someday.

Although Anthony and Annamarie didn't have their father's marvelously thick Italian accent, they did have his marvelously thick, black hair. When Mr. Milano taught the congregation his songs with gusto and charismatic warmth, his children grew brighter, stars in his constellation. They were, in the parlance of neighborhoods and churches, The Milanos.

The Milanos, as with some of the other core families who came to church, were the blood and bone of our Mennonite meetinghouse. The adults ate the communion bread that my mother had baked. They drank Welch's Grape juice that had been in our fridge that morning. We sang songs together, ate fellowship meals together. We opened the living room door, and there were the people. Just like the finger play, that was us. That was our house. That was our church. We were all part of the family of God.

So, even though I distanced myself from this time, when my dad called and said he had bad news about Anthony, they were bringing news about a family member.

Anthony, as it turned out, had been stabbed to death.

Dad explained that Anthony had gone to a bar, and two men wouldn't leave him alone. They wanted to rough someone up.

He paused, then, not sure how much to say. I didn't know how to respond. I felt like I might be sick.

"The men are in custody now," he said.

The men were alive, and Anthony was dead.

I asked about his family. I wondered about Annamarie—they were practically twins. Then we hung up. I sat in the telephone stall of my dorm floor, staring through the glass at a fire extinguisher across the hall. In my mind's eye, Anthony was still a teenager with gentle black eyes and a mischievous grin. We were swimming in his pool, and he was throwing me a ball.

Soon the news came that he was gay, and in fact the men had been teasing him all night and forced him to take them home. Of course, he would never reach their home—or his own. The hate behind this kind of action was incomprehensible to me.

I turned, as I did with much of what I was dealing with at college, to writing poetry. I spent hours trying to work out Anthony's death in the repetitions of a villanelle. Jonathan was in the poetry class, and I talked with him about the real Anthony behind the poem, but only in an abstract way. I didn't know how to grieve, far away from Levittown and from home.

In my poem, I kept returning to the image of blood in the snow. It was an image of innocence lost, not only his but my own. I wrote, "I feel the knocking on my wrists, Anthony."

I'd never thought about suicide before. But my body was whirring with rage and grief, and I could not express it beyond my lines of poetry. Anthony had been different, just as I was different. As a gay man, he fit in neither with the Mennonite culture we grew up in nor with large parts of society. I felt that I was a misfit, too. I just hadn't been found out yet. In one phone call, the world was just as shifty as it had been when I believed the Lord would rapture us at any moment. Each day could go either way—it was a total crapshoot. Beautiful, gentle Anthony was gone.

I tried wading through this with Ingrid, knowing that it sounded like a poor explanation for being an absent friend.

"I'm sorry," I concluded. "I wasn't myself then."

"Okay," Ingrid said, grumbling a little.

"I called you now."

"I know."

We made a plan. As soon as I could get the money together, I'd take a Greyhound bus to Tennessee.

7

A Fair Trade

*A*unt Sandi's summer-pool-blue eyes were sparkling as she handed me a blue airmail envelope with postage from France.

"You might want this—it's about time, huh?"

We were standing in her kitchen as I took the envelope, the Dutch blue cabinets and white floor appearing much more spacious and angelic than just moments before.

"I guess so!" I said, breathless from running up the basement stairs. The envelope seemed to be stuffed with many pages. "You'll have to excuse me."

She nodded knowingly.

I tore it open and began to read on my way down the stairs to my room.

"So Cynthia," he began. He was in Paris. He'd gotten my letters. I scanned over his musings on Paris sight-seeing and boisterous Americans, his comments on the art of letter writing, and Prince's latest album. I wanted to know where his heart was. Finally, on page 5, I read:

"You mentioned that you no longer need me for your happiness. Yes, it does sound harsh, but I agree with you that it's a positive development. Before I left for my trip I realized the enviable state of my position and I didn't like it—I felt wary. Enviable in that I felt so much loved and needed by you. I was wary because I thought it was possible we were embarking on the same cycle that brought about the destruction of our relationship. In other words, I was concerned that it could only go downhill from there with you coming to the realization, once again, that I wasn't all that great, indispensable after all.

"I realized that by removing myself for a year you would inevitably grow more independent from me. I realize I risk losing you completely (as you wrote: you don't need me for your happiness) but, if I have to lose you, I'd rather lose you now than 5-10 yrs. from now when the disillusionment or whatever hits again."

He signed his letter, "I love this girl, Jonathan."

He had a point. The best thing to do was to live one moment at a time, and live it as best as we could, taking us to God-knows-where. He had a point, but I don't think I got it right away, because his ink was smearing from drops of tears, my head crowded by risk factors and chances of further disillusionment.

When Aunt Sandi asked about the letter later, I explained that he still had a lot of traveling to do, and that I still had a lot of work to do. She and Uncle Roy knew why he was keeping his distance, and yet they still wondered how long it was going to last. "I wonder what's so interesting in Europe," she mused.

I told her about his wanderlust, a part of him I was drawn to but now wondered if it would keep him abroad forever. Jonathan had spent his first six years in Somalia, home of many nomads. (His best friend in college was a nomadic Somali named Mohammed.) Then changes in the political climate forced his family to leave, and they moved to Kenya. Jonathan felt more at home abroad than in the United States, I knew that, but I also knew he was very attached to his family, all of whom were now in the States.

"I think he'll return," I told Sandi, trying to convince myself more than her.

Jonathan's better points were returning to me, now that I was cleaning up the mess of my internal life. I adored his long hair, lush eyelashes, dangly earrings. The way he wore eye makeup to go out dancing. In college, I had to have an ex-girlfriend of his confirm for me that he wasn't gay. I had loved his style—I saw myself as outside of gender restrictions, too. He served me drinks when I went to his house. I butched up my hair and stopped shaving my legs. He wore a *macaawiis*, a Somali skirt for men. I was sure he was like my mother. Except my mother didn't wear makeup.

Goshen was our halfway house to the world. Although it was a Mennonite college, there were some professors there who had come of age in the 1960s and were urbane, global-thinking. And there were students, like me, who wanted to experiment with different ways of being. Like being drunk. Or being radical feminists. There was one guy who wore a skirt to school for a day, just to see what would happen. Nothing happened. It was Goshen College, 1988. Freaks were okay.

Jonathan and I were like proton and electron to each other. We sped on his motorcycle through cornfield country; we danced barefoot until we were sweaty and sore; we smoked under the moon, talking about the Wheel of Life. I broke up with him three times before we moved to New York. I loved him, yet I kept coming up empty. But this time was different. I had torn our friendship beyond the pale.

◆

Betts was quilting in the morning, so I made one last attempt with the video camera, planting it on a tripod across from her in her dining room. Betts sat before an oval frame that

> Mar. 10, 1936. Beautiful day. Who doesn't like these days after such a cold winter. I made ice cream today. It may be the last chance because the ice is going fast.

held the patchwork she was quilting. Behind her was the grand-father clock, watching over her work with a steady gaze.

I trained the video on her, happy to hide myself behind a camera. After reading Jonathan's letter, I wasn't in the mood to do much interviewing. Then Betts got up abruptly and went over to the television. She came back with her blue crocheted bonnet.

"Now I'll look like a little Mennonite lady," she said with a giggle. She sat back down before the frame.

In any story, there is fiction, a made-up element. She'd just added a piece.

"I don't think I made any for Kris yet," she said, referring to her plan of making a quilt for each of the seventeen grandchildren. "And the others. I have to get them made."

"You will," I said. "At the rate you're going." She'd already made at least a dozen quilts in her retirement years.

Being with my grandparents was very grounding. They knew what they wanted, and that was the simple life they were living on the Hill with each other and their family. Nothing truly unsettling happened here, unless you were a squirrel rights activist.

"Well, quilting—I've been at it for four weeks," Betts said. "But making patches is what takes so long."

"Does Grandpop ever help you quilt?" I asked. Henry was reading the newspaper in the living room.

"No!" she emphasizes. "Some men cut patches, some retired men, but Grandpop's not interested. Where are you, Daddy?"

"Here," was his reply from the other end of the room.

"Why don't you come here?"

"I don't know if you want me on it," he answered, gesturing toward me.

"Grandpop!" I chided him.

"Well!" said Betts.

She tried luring him with flattery: "I don't know how these things work, Daddy. Why don't you come out here?"

He began to get up, and so Betts relaxed and asked me about my job situation. I told her that I had a freelance article due about a restaurant near Allentown, and that after that I wasn't sure.

"Maybe you'll have to work at McDonald's," she concluded. I couldn't tell if she was kidding or not.

"No," I said. "Not McDonald's."

"Well you can find some other kind of job."

The work ethic book I had stored opened up again before me—"unproductive," "leech." The headings were in bold.

I slammed it shut, watched the dust fly.

"This is a job," I said, nodding to my video camera. "I just don't get paid for it."

"Well, what are you doing tomorrow, then?"

"That's a good question," I said. "I don't know." I asked if we could keep going with our interviews, but she said, "What do you have to do yet? We could finish today. I have to get an afghan done, too, till we have our bazaar." Their Christmas bazaar at church raised money for charity.

"Now look at that tree out there!" Betts exclaimed suddenly, looking out through the bay window and pointing. "It was so pretty, and now it's just all bare."

I was thinking about Jonathan's letter, how he had said that he loved me. He didn't trust me, but he loved me. I suppose I felt the same way. I loved him, but I was afraid that I was one of those people others described as "not the marrying kind." My own emptiness kept me from loving well.

The quilting was put away; Betts was back in her stuffed chair by the bay window. Henry had on a bolo tie he'd picked up decades before in Arizona when visiting his son Henry Paul.

Mar. 12. 1936. I was helping Ada quilt her Dutch grill quilt. This eve. we were at cooking school.

He fingered the worn leather strings as he spoke.

"We had a house on Hall Street in Allentown. I was working at Pop's store. When the Great Depression came, the bank was shrewd enough to select certain property owners who were paid up on their taxes, and said you had to furnish the balance of the mortgage within thirty days. I owed thirty-nine hundred dollars on the property, and I didn't have that much."

Henry crossed his legs. "Not many people had thirty-nine hundred dollars in those days. So the bank took the property. This particular bank seemed to specialize in that.

"That's a crime," I protested

"Well, that was the law," Henry shrugged.

"Lots of people lost their places," Betts interjected.

"The banks were shrewd enough to select those not back on their taxes," Henry repeated. "People were out of work, see, and they couldn't pay their taxes. But the bank selected those whose taxes were paid—I was one of them. That way when they foreclosed on a property, they didn't owe any taxes."

Henry reflected a moment, then continued. "I remember having an argument with my pop. I worked in his store. It was on 723 St. John Street. We sold bread and baked goods, sausage and canned goods, produce, and other things. People at the store would buy on credit. I told Pop, 'We can't afford credit.' I said, 'Let's tell people they'll have to pay cash from now on.' But Pop was afraid they wouldn't come at all.

"That was when these bigger grocery stores like we have now were starting in, and people would go there for their shopping. But 'Yeah,' I said, 'if they buy on credit and they lose their job, we would lose the money anyway.' He said, 'I never talked to my dad that way, and I don't think it's right that you talk to me that way.' I said, 'I'm not talking to you as Dad. I'm talking to you as business partner.'

"And that's what happened. There was a family of five across the street—the man lost his job and they had no income. We didn't want to see the children go hungry, so we canceled their bill at the store. Then the man died—and we canceled the second bill. And that's how it went, canceling bills, and there wasn't enough to support my pop and me both." He tapped his fingertips together.

"Wow, that's a shame," I said, but then wasn't sure if it was. His father had fed some hungry families, but my grandfather lost his job over it. It was certainly bad business sense.

"I got out," Henry continued, "and Betts and I moved to Bally. I took a job as a huckster for my Uncle William, selling meat products in the winter—sausage, scrapple—and asparagus in the summer."

Henry reviewed their various moves, from his uncle Abraham Gehman's farm, now a golf course and airport, to a house on Arland Longacre's farm, then finally to a place of their own.

"My uncle Harvey Ruth and his neighbor, Ulysses Moyer, said they'd remodel the chicken house at Betts' pop's place for us. They spent a lot of time renovating that chicken house before we moved in."

He tapped his fingers on his armrests. "I often thought I should've taken a picture, a before and after, but film cost a quarter. And I didn't have a quarter."

Betts was shaking her head, looking a little weary. "Not then," she said.

"They didn't charge us any money for the work," Henry continued. "They did it out of the goodness of their heart, just to help a fellow out. I often think back—how did I ever repay them anything but a thank you?

"After the place was renovated," Henry went on, "it was forty-eight feet long, by twenty-two wide."

Mar. 29, 1936. Today Harold is four years old. Henry Paul's eyes are very sore yet with the measles. Arland's children have them, too. The doctor was here for the last time today. He was here nine times.

Betts added, "And it had a lot of windows around. We called it Dogwood Cottage. It had a nice size kitchen and a living room and three bedrooms. They weren't that big, though. But there we lived with the five boys, for what? Twelve years was it? I don't know what we paid, two or five dollars a month for rent. They made it real nice, but in the summer, if it got too hot, well, you'd know it was a chicken house." She grimaced.

Henry swiveled a little in his chair.

"We had no phone up there," Betts continued. "Henry wasn't earning enough and we had five children. My parents had a phone. They lived in the main house. When we finally got a phone, that was in the forties, after we moved to a bigger place, down here," Betts said, gesturing down the hill. "Rich was just about three or four. It was around Christmas time, and he came out to the kitchen and said, 'I know what your Christmas present is. I can't tell you what it is. But when it rings, you'll hear it.'

"It's torn down now, Dogwood Cottage. But the main house is there, where my pop used to live. If you go, up behind the pond, you can still see the foundation stones. It was cold, that house. We had a kitchen range to heat the kitchen and a parlor heater that burned coal. But the bedrooms were cold."

Betts was crossing her arms, and her ankles, as if still feeling the chill. "Oh, yeah. I'll tell you how cold it was. You know the twins wet their cribs at night. And then when they'd wake, I'd take them to the kitchen to dress them and wash them by the warmth of the kitchen range. By the time I'd return to their room to get the wet pads out, and to make their beds, why the pads were froze. They were froze! Yeah, that's how cold it was.

"But we had someone who knew us real well at The Rock Hill Sewing Circle. She had the ladies make some covers for the cribs. And we had running water all the time because there was a spring up at my dad's place, just above our Dogwood Cottage. The spring ran all the time, so it didn't freeze, see. That was our drinking water and we used it for washing, too."

Betts paused to rub her eye under her glasses.

"The outhouse was kind of scary in the dark," she continued. "I always thought about snakes. But not like down at the Longacre farm where we first lived. There we had copperheads. Everybody, most of our friends and all," Betts said, smoothing her dress over her lap, "they were living the way we did."

"Talk Daddy," she said abruptly. Henry was sitting quietly, staring at his folded hands. He looked up, shrugged his shoulders, and gave a little smile.

"We helped each other," Betts continued, turning back to me. "You know, if our children couldn't wear their clothing anymore, we gave it to somebody who could. Goodness—how would children nowadays live through something like that? Now it all has to match. In those days, we just wore what we had. Other people couldn't buy expensive clothes either. They just didn't have the money."

I enlisted Henry at this point. He cleared his throat and swiveled a little. I noticed through the window that it had begun to drizzle. Some clouds thinned to light gray patches between the darker ones.

Henry said, "We traded. I used to sell asparagus house-to-house in the summertime—plus asparagus and whatever few vegetables we had to sell. And meat in the wintertime in Pennsburg. Once I saw this stove for sale. I told the lady, I'm selling meat. So I made arrangements with her. I said, 'I'll buy this. After I've sold enough meat, I'll fetch it.' That's the way we got

---

Nov. 14, 1937. I am mending thirds for Gehman's Factory[3] this winter, it's all I can get to do at home just now. I don't like to mend very much. I get 5 ¢ to do a dozen pair. I do 30 doz. a week. Arland got the agency for the Bendix home laundry, a new invention in washing, so Henry, Jim, and Abram went down to Phila. to learn how they are put together and how to repair them.

our kitchen stove, and a lot of things. Shoes. When we needed shoes, I'd go to a fella and tell him, 'I have meat [and I have this and so on and so on], and I need shoes.' 'Okay,' he'd say. And then we'd trade. Lard—we slaughtered pigs, so there was the lard. We traded lard for tires. It was a fair exchange."

My grandparents were resourceful. This explained something about my own childhood regarding waste: how could you throw out a plate of uneaten lima beans when just a generation ago, those beans were cash?

"What happened to the store?" I asked, recalling some rumor of unsettled accounts.

"I actually never heard what happened to Pop's store," Henry said.

"We won't go into that. We never did," Betts said flatly.

"It was sold, though," I asked, tentatively.

"If you turn off that thing," Betts said, pointing to my tape recorder, "then I'll tell you what happened."

I clicked "stop."

"See," Betts said, "when Henry's mother died, just after he was born, there was an inheritance. And that went to the three boys. They each were given nine hundred dollars, but Henry's stepmother thought it should've gone to Henry's pop—Henry, Sr. She had two girls, you know, and of course they didn't get any of the inheritance."

"Pop," Henry explained, "was farming and he needed the money, too, I guess. Anyhow, Mom thought that Pop should've received the money. But with that money, we boys bought partnership in Pop's store."

"She never forgot that," Betts said, wagging a finger. "We never saw what happened to the store. None of the boys were working there anymore, but they still had partnerships."

I asked if they knew anything—even a scrap about it.

"We found out later," Betts said, and there was indignation in her blue eyes. "Henry's brother Norman went to the courthouse, and saw the store had been sold by Henry's brother-in-law. His step-sister's husband. I don't think they got much for it. But enough to buy themselves a house."

Henry added, in a conciliatory tone, "We always said we're on good terms. If we fuss about this, we'll likely disagree, and become like so many families."

I listened for an edge in his voice, almost hoping I'd find some resentment, some sense of outrage. But there was none. Betts said plainly, "But Norman and Henry, they didn't see any of the money from their partnership."

Jan. 11, 1938. This was my birthday. I'm thirty years old already.

8

Left Behind

When I was living in New York, Betts did something very simple that altered my life. She sent me a poem that I had written at age eight. It was on that thin, watermarked typing paper that my father had used on his old Smith-Corona. It was dated in my grandfather's pen, "November 11, 1974." The poem is unremarkable, the last stanza made up of the stuff of living with a cat and dog in the house:

If I'd ever find a rat,
I'd feed it to my cat,
And if she would choke it up,
I would feed it to my pup.

Henry and Betts had a rolltop desk full of files and note-books and old bookkeeping records, the safe house for this poem over those fifteen years. I felt that I'd received a relic from a ship that I had long ago abandoned. I'd thought that my writing emerged as an adult, a vocation born out of angst and des-peration. I wondered if I'd ever get over it, like an illness. I'd completely forgotten that I'd written poems when I was eight, in elementary school, when pet vomit was the most pressing thing.

For someone like me who had daily and sometimes hourly shifts in what I thought I should do with my life—shifts that included becoming a physical therapist, a radio announcer, and an archaeologist—the fact that I was a poet at age eight—no matter how bad a poet—was a life-altering realization. Writing was the thread that was constant in my life, while everything else (my geography, my beliefs, my circle of friends, my hair) had changed. Of course, it was becoming clearer to me now—I shouldn't be beating my head against the wall because my elementary school students are throwing paper balls at each other. I should be a writer.

This knowledge of my early vocation confirmed what I had been doing since I was a child. If I ever felt overwhelmed by a situation, I would just place myself outside myself and observe. I had come to see this as writerly observation. Another description might be dissociating. In the Mennonite tradition I was raised in, we were all simultaneously insiders and outsiders. We learned early that we lived in the world, but we were not of the world. As a child, I was taught the very specific applications to this: no cartoons, no card-playing; no revealing clothes; no makeup; no rock 'n roll; no dancing; no Santa Claus; no Christmas tree; no Tooth Fairy; no Halloween witches. And, most important of all, no skipping church ever—even on vacation. We were so not-of-the-world that it wasn't bad news that at any moment, Jesus could appear in the clouds to sweep us up to heaven.

Some months after this poem came in the mail, I was reading my more recent, vomitless poems in open-mike cafés in the Village. As I stood behind the lectern one night, holding onto its edges, I noticed something about the people in the audience. There was the middle-aged man, with a sagging belly, who'd just read a poem about his father's post-whiskey beatings. A woman a little older than me with a pockmarked face and short, feathery hair, had performed a poem about incest. Another woman who looked like she'd been up all night crying, and had on lots of makeup to compensate, was sitting in the back corner, listening. As I looked around, I saw Levittown

Mennonite Meetinghouse. Our church, our family of God, had its share of broken people seeking to put themselves back together again—or at least trying to survive. I saw myself looking through my dad's eyes, looking over the lectern to the congregation. My face flushed. I finished my poem and sat down.

This was my first stroll through the twenty-something realm in which you discover how little of your own person you actually are and how much like your family you've become. Of course there was a difference between what my dad did and what I did. In his church, they praised God. In my open-mike church, we didn't talk about God, either because we didn't think God had much to do with anything, or we thought that God had everything to do with everything, and so there was no point in talking about it. In either case, the end of the world was not my concern. I had planted my feet so firmly on the ground, no one would ever rapture me, not even Jesus himself.

There was a good reason for this. To me, the reason is encapsulated in this childhood story:

Once in elementary school, I returned home from school to our Levittown Mennonite Meetinghouse, and no one was around. The cat was out back, flicking her tail at the birds, but no humans were anywhere to be found.

"Mom," I yelled, running up the staircase. "Mom, I'm home."

My bedroom was empty. My mom's bedroom was empty. The bathroom, empty.

"Mom. Are you here?"

I bolted down the stairs and out to the back porch.

"Mom?" Now my body was everywhere hot and cold at the same time.

I ran all the way around the house, still dragging my book bag with me. And then it hit me, when I reached the back door again. It all became crystal clear. They talked about it in Sunday school all of the time. Of course—Jesus had returned in the clouds and had taken my mother.

I looked at the clouds, and they were a gray blanket. Why hadn't I heard the trumpets? The neighbor's house seemed still, like it had been evacuated.

"Mom," I cried, not expecting an answer now.

I ran for the phone. I could hardly breathe. I dialed Ingrid's number, a number I knew because we talked on the phone all the time.

Ingrid's older sister answered.

I could hardly talk because I was sobbing too much.

Her mom got on the phone.

"Calm down," she said. "Stop crying and tell me what's wrong."

"I. Can't. Find. My. Mom."

She said she'd be right over.

I put the phone back in its cradle and ran to the couch. I sat, hiding in my knees, wondering if we'd all been left behind. Of course, if Jesus had taken my mom, then he probably took my dad, and my sister, and . . . and . . .

The front screen door banged. I didn't dare to move.

My mom was walking toward me.

"Mom!"

I ran to her and held her fast. She was just over at the neighbor's house, she said. Sorry it got later than expected. That must have scared you, coming home to an empty house . . .

Some people are more laid back about their belief in Jesus returning *at any time*, but I was a very literal child. There are a million reasons I could choose from for not believing in the rapture, but for me it's simple: Death is one of the basic laws of the universe. The rat is fed to the cat. Why make it more scary than it already is? How is that better than watching the *Texas Chainsaw Massacre*?

◆

Irony has a way of creeping around people and playing silly tricks. As a citizen of Kulp Hill, there was an unstated assumption that I would attend church. That church turned out to be my grandparents' rather conservative Mennonite church, run by a minister who personified for me End Times eschatology.

Every year I'd gone to summer camp, Al Detweiler conducted altar calls in front of a roaring fire, in the dimly lit pavilion of Spruce Lake Wilderness Camp. Al was a friend of my parents, a bear of a figure with full and shining white hair, broad shoulders, and a booming bass voice that could crack boulders. He reminded me of Charlton Heston in *The Ten Commandments* after he sees the burning bush: his face is ruddy, his hair swept back, eyes ignited.

When Al saw me walk into the foyer with Betts, he reached out and gave me a tight hug, which was his customary greeting. This time, however, I was bigger. My feet didn't leave the floor.

"Well, is it Cindi Yoder?" he asked rhetorically, his deep voice lined with the familiar rasp at its edge. He said Cindi Yoder the same way I would have said Al Detweiler, if I'd said his full name. It's the way you name someone from the past, a figure come back to life, as surprising as Lazarus.

"I'm here with Grammie and Grandpop. I'm living on the Hill for a while."

"Well, they should feel lucky to have you," he said, winking at my grandmother. I gave him an update on my parents. Then it was time for church, and I sat down with my grandparents in their pew.

When Al took the lectern, it was only a moment before I was back at the campfire, all preteen wonder. After Al gave his talk to the campers, we sang songs that worked us up for the altar call. The one that seemed to be the favorite—we sang it all the time—was a Larry Norman song about children dying and being trampled down by war and people being snatched away from you—and if only you were ready when Jesus came down and raptured all of the good people, none of this would have happened. The song was bad enough, but after watching too many rapture movies with my church's youth group, it also conjured up images of slacker Christians lined up at the guillotine.

I was eight, nine, ten, eleven. Each year, I got down from my bench and stood tall under Al's protective, outstretched arms and confessed my sins. I was very clear on this—I was not going to lose my head.

Sitting safely now on a pew, I shuddered from the memory and did a trick I used to do as a child during religious moments when I wished I were somewhere else: I pulled myself out to a place slightly above center, and became an observer.

I observed how the very same white lock of hair flipped forward over Al's forehead when he emphasized a point. How Henry fell asleep. How a woman next to me kept craning her neck to look around. I wished Mennonite churches would have something more interesting to look at behind the lectern than a wooden cross. I longed to go over and open the opaque window at the end of my pew so that I could see out. We sat at the same spot, on the same bench as when I was a little girl, wishing I had some of the "church candy" Grammie used to give me: Sweetarts or peppermints.

Weeks later, sitting in that same spot, my hymnal cracked open on my lap, I heard myself sing a song about God's love. I heard myself sing the words, *God's love,* and I looked at the self that was above my body, observing, and at the self that had just heard a thing that sounded true, and I realized that I wasn't really here at all. I had divided myself into two neat parts: the person who behaved as if she were here, and the person who had left her body and was far away, dancing on the other side of the moon.

Surrounded by the waves of congregational singing, I felt arms of grief wrap around me. I had spent a lot of time wandering around looking for truth, when it was right before me. I felt that I'd come around to the starting point of a wide, gaping circle. Not that the guillotine was truth for me, or trumpets and earth-evacuation, but there was certainly love here—Al was a big bear-ful of love—and openness to the divine that I had wrapped up with the bad rapture flicks and tossed away.

Alone later in my apartment, I recalled what my friend Patrick had asked about whether I wrote instead of actually living, and it cut to the bone, a truth that was white and hard. I had to get back into my body again.

I cued up the Smiths on my turntable and lit some candles, and danced on my cold floor, spinning in circles, getting into the kind of surrender that we used to get into at the altar, when we saved our souls, when the fire flickered dry and hot—the kind of surrender where we just forget about everything except that one moment, when we know our souls are saved and we know for certain that if we die the next morning, we will not plummet but will be caught by the hands of God.

It's the kind of surrender I got into when I was a teenager, after a Jesus festival, when I'd play my contemporary Christian music, and dance around the living room, singing *He's coming back, He's coming back to take me Home*, offering myself up so that Jesus would take me and save me from my awkward teenage life.

Only this time, I wasn't going anywhere.

So I danced, and it was a kind of stripping, a loss of interiors and exteriors. I spun, the vibration of the music loosening everything around me, making it lose form. I danced for an hour, maybe more, maybe less. I danced until I was not a writer or a granddaughter or a daughter or a woman. I was not a depressed person or a Mennonite or an estranged spouse. I wasn't separate or different or crazy. Or I was all of these things, and none of it mattered. I was a lone figure shaking in the soul of the universe. One blessed, crackling flame in the soul of God, Allah, Yahweh or whatever name people give to the soul that holds us. I was a flame dancing in my sweaty, fire-lit skin, dancing on a worn gray carpet, in a cold room in winter.

9

Red Hot Pokers

A postcard came from Jonathan. The picture was of an ancient gravestone in Prague, and his note was cryptic—a note about his visit to the graveyard and about his plans to go to Africa. It was like a travelog entry, with no mention of my last letter. Shredding it was the first thing that came to mind. But the image of the gravestone, shaped round like a face, stopped me. I tacked it up on the bulletin board over my typewriter. It reminded me of what had, at one time, worked between us. On our invitations to our wedding reception on Memorial Day weekend, we'd drawn two gravestones:

Jonathan Shenk	Cynthia Yoder
Single	Single
1966-1989	1966-1989

We thought it was funny. Then one of Jonathan's conservative uncles wrote to us, reprimanding us for making sport of a sacred event. Not surprisingly, he didn't show up for the party.

◆

Snow covered the three wooden steps between my aunt and uncle's house and my grandparents' place. Hurrying a little, I tripped up the steps, catching myself from going headlong with my papers and tape recorder on the soggy steps. It was still

snowing, and I bent forward, sheltering my journalist's wares with my body. Inside their apartment, I unloaded my bundle on the sofa, and left my jacket by the fireplace.

"Well," Betts remarked, "I wasn't planning on going anywhere special today. It's a good day to stay in, not?"

"Yes, not," I said.

Betts offered me some Christmas cookies, which she'd made for our upcoming family gathering. Christmas for this family was about feasting, talking, hymn-singing, and playing table games like *Monopoly.* The feast tradition was that all of the courses were served together, so that no one had to sit in agony over their ham, wondering if the Bavarian cream was gone, or if someone had taken the last piece of minced meat pie.

I nibbled on the sugar cookies while taking notes. I asked her about having six children.

"The children—I knew they'd come," Betts said, her hands folded in her lap. "At that time, we didn't have any preventative, like they do now. Pills and such. All of our friends had children soon."

I wasn't expecting to talk about birth control. She loved her children fiercely. But there it was: she was of childbearing age during a time when access to prophylactics in an insulated Mennonite community was limited.

Henry adjusted his new hearing aid, a sticking point between Betts and him. Being the social butterfly that she was, Betts couldn't stand the thought that Henry could turn conver-

July 4, 1942. Had the Gehman reunion at Henry Schantz's farm. There were 80 present. Harvey Ruths' treated all the children to a half pt. ice cream. In the afternoon we all went in the barn where they had a program. It consisted of singing, Carol & Bernie played on the marimba, Daddy had a topic, "Facing the Times." Nelson Moyer showed pictures, and at last a spelling bee.

sations on and off with a switch. Since Henry was an electrician whose primary interest in life was fiddling with gadgets, I thought it was fitting that he'd have this on his ear, his very own gadget that he could manipulate according to whim.

"When we lived down at the Gehman farm," Betts said, "Henry Paul was already born and Harold was born there. And Daddy, you were getting a dollar a day at Longacres. You'd walk all the way up from that farm to Bally."

Henry nodded in agreement.

"But we only paid five dollars a month rent at that place," Betts said.

"Milk was six cents a quart," Henry added.

"We got by," Betts said, "We don't have many pictures of Harold when he was little, because we didn't have money to buy film for the camera. We have a few of him, but not very many. Not until Henry Paul got a camera, but that was after the Depression had ended.

"We used to garden there at Gehman's. We had a patch out back where we planted corn and other things. And we had so many cherries there that year. Cherries were plentiful. We canned a lot of cherries. The Gehman's grew asparagus—an acre at least—and we used to help with that. We had to cut it every morning and evening, that's how fast it grew.

"Yeah, and we had a little creek running down there. We put a water wheel in it to make our own electric. But it wasn't a strong creek, and in the summer, it would dry up. So we didn't have electric in the summer."

"A lot of things were rationed during the war," Betts continued. "Sugar, butter, shoes. You couldn't buy shoes. You had to have a stamp book for that. We have some of the books yet. You'd tear a stamp out from them—and had to have a good reason. Sugar was the main thing that bothered us. We did a lot of canning and couldn't get sugar unless we had a stamp. I got more than Mom did because of our children. I'd give her some; then maybe she'd give it back. That way, you'd shift."

Betts paused, leaning forward. "Daddy, you're not talking."

"I don't have anything to say," Henry responded with a little bemused smile,

"Sure you do," she said. "Your brother Norman remembers a lot of things."

Henry said, "Well?"

Betts prodded him. "Well, remember you used to coast?"

Henry gave in.

"Okay," he said, clearing his throat. "Gas they rationed, too. And we'd turn off the car and coast down the hill here to get to church. You saved on your gas that way. And I walked to work. A mile each way."

Betts sat back, satisfied.

"At that time," Betts went on, "we would invite men in the Civilian Public Service for Sunday dinner. A lot of those CPS fellows worked up in Allentown in a state hospital, and when we went up to Allentown to church, we would bring them back to our place at Dogwood Cottage."

Civilian Public Service was an alternative to fighting in the war. Many Mennonites were conscientious objectors, following the church's creed of peaceful nonresistance.

"We didn't know too many people in the war. Not many Mennonites went," she continued. "I know one man from our church was in the military, but while he was in he studied some more, and he found that it was wrong. He got out then. He had quite a time, but he got out. We still write to those CPS fellows, out in Kansas and Wisconsin and Oklahoma—different ones."

None of my family members, going back as long as anyone can remember, fought in any wars. My dad, Ray, and his twin, Roy, opted for alternative service in Arizona with migrant workers during the Korean War. That was our culture. When I

Mar. 27, 1943. Henry took Henry Paul along for the last time to market. People almost tore each other apart for meat.

was a teen, my heroes were people who had gone to prison for protesting the draft during Vietnam. I, and many of my peers, joined a conference-wide effort to collect personal statements about our convictions on nonviolence. I typed up my statement on my dad's Smith-Corona and filed it with the Franconia Mennonite Conference, the governing body of the Mennonite churches in that area. When I left the Mennonite tradition as a young adult, it was the one belief I kept.

The next day, I walked up Kulp Hill toward the crest. Where the road rises above the woods, you can turn and look over a valley that on a clear day goes mile upon mile. On this morning, the valley was covered with snow. I checked if I could see as far as the Limerick Nuclear Power Plant. There was something both beautiful and repulsive about the gusts of steam, the concrete hourglass cooling towers.

On the way back down, it happened again. The streaks of tar that were slapped over cracks in the road formed themselves into sinister shapes, with eyes and nasty-looking mouths. I thought I was over this. I stopped, and stared back. I let my eyes move along the shape of the tar, seeing the material for what it was. I took a deep breath, wondering what was scaring me.

Maybe it was the cooling towers and my fear of nuclear annihilation, held over from the cold war. Or maybe it was just basic fear, arising out of no specific place, a rootless fear. I said hello to the familiar face of fear and walked home.

◆

Henry was turning the dial on the radio when I entered the living room. Seeing my sweat pants and shirt, Betts asked me if I'd gone up the hill. She was always interested in whether I took my walk or not.

"I saw the cooling towers," I said.

"Oh, yeah. I don't much like them," she said. She was fingering one of several handkerchiefs she kept tucked into the side of her chair. The edges of the handkerchief were crocheted in pink. She added, still thinking about my walk, "When we were living at Dogwood Cottage, the children would walk all the way down to where the Longacre Dairy is. And they'd walk out there at night to go skating, like Henry and I used to."

"That's probably over a mile," I said, sitting down on the davenport. She was cutting off dead leaves from some of her plants in the bay window.

"Yeah, that's right. That was during gas rationing, during the war, and we didn't have the gas to take them. We had blackouts, too. We used to always say, 'What would they do if there'd be an air raid?'"

She went to the kitchen to throw out the leaves, and returned to sit in her chair. "Except for the war, it wasn't dangerous for youngsters to walk along the road, like it is now. Now it isn't safe in the daytime or any time at all. Yeah, that's why I always say I'm glad we raised our children when we did."

She handed me a postcard from my cousin, Tonya, Uncle Roy and Aunt Sandi's daughter. Tonya was a little younger than me, but much taller, with Sandi's intense blue eyes and her father's softish voice. In the way Mennonites tend to travel in packs, we'd ended up at the same Mennonite college, and she was now completing her Study Service Trimester in China.

"She wrote home for the recipe for Pig's Stomach," Betts said, clearly delighted. "She wanted to make it for some people she knows there. I wrote it to her, but I don't know if she can buy the stomach there." She chuckled. "I guess she'll go to the market and see what she can find."

The image popped into my mind of a man I'd passed on the street in Chinatown. He had an entire dead pig on his shoulder.

"I'm sure she'll find something," I assured her.

> April 7, 1943. I did my mending this forenoon, and this afternoon I worked in the factory. This evening I cut a seersucker dress.

"We were talking about children," Betts continued. "Well, I say if you can't talk things out, there's a bigger problem there. Not only on Donahue, but this Oprah—she had mothers and daughters on. They wouldn't even talk to each other."

Henry had turned off the radio, and leaned back far into his chair, folding his hands over his waist. He was wearing his brown corduroy slippers.

He said, "We always insisted on things we thought were right. For instance, when we got television, and the children wanted to watch programs we didn't think appropriate, I took the television to work. Or when they rode a bike and did something they weren't supposed to do, I'd put a chain on the bike."

Betts slapped her thigh, laughing. "The children used to complain that these were dumb ways to punish them, and Henry would say, 'What do you want me to do—give you an ice-cream cone?'"

Henry added, "I raised them the way I thought was right. Not to say I didn't make mistakes."

"Nowadays, there's more freedom in general," Betts said, "of doing your own thing. But there's so much violence.

"I have to tell you this one story," she said, changing her tone. "My mother had some flowers called Red-Hot Pokers. These flowers had straight stalks, and the tops were beautiful and red and pointed, just like—well, that poker by the stove.

"My mother had a wonderful flower garden. She had peonies and all these annuals, you know. She'd go out to Lancaster, and her friends would give plants to her. She'd have that whole garden, just in flowers. And the twins, well, we were living in Dogwood Cottage, and they'd get into things. These Red-Hot Pokers, the twins went up into her garden and picked all of them off! They bloomed rarely, not every year, and here the boys had picked them all." Betts added with a little laugh, "This was the only time I smacked the twins."

♦

Henry and Betts were observing their sixty-fifth wedding anniversary. They celebrated, as they usually celebrated life events, with friends and family at the social hall of their church. I was nervous to attend this gathering, embarrassed to be alone, knowing that everyone would be wondering what was up with Jonathan but that no one would ask.

During tributes to my grandparents, I read from some of the stories I was collecting. Even though I was trying to keep irony out of my writing, trying to be more open and reflective, it felt strange to show them their lives as I had written them on the page. After running so far away from my family's values and their way of life, here I was, clinging to my grandparents' every word, making their lives my own in the funny way a writer sometimes becomes what he or she writes.

The old stone house where Betts grew up, and where she married my grandfather still stands, and since many family members were around for the anniversary, some of us took the occasion for a walk up the Hill. The house has an epic quality, having been the house where my great-grandfather brought his family when Betts was a girl. And later on, it was where they'd converted the chicken house to Dogwood Cottage. The walk wasn't far from my grandparents' place, a small distance through the woods. Some of my cousins, aunts, and uncles made the trek up the road, rounding the bend to find a few sheep standing near the shallow pond on the property.

The chicken coop house is gone; just foundation stones are left. We stopped in to drink from the tin cup that hung above the spring near the house. We had a funny communion, passing the cup, filled at this ancient spring, that was there when my grandmother was a girl—and earlier. The water was cold, and

May 5, 1943. This eve. the Bally folks organized a sewing circle at Ruths Haven as they cannot get gas to go to Pottstown [Church]. Twenty-seven were present.

the chill of the tin was jarring against my lips. An artist, Allan Eitzen, who lived at the house, was a friend of the family and came out to talk. I wished that Dogwood Cottage still stood. But such a structure wouldn't last. It was built for chickens.

◆

Friday was pie night. Betts put out a display of homemade pie and boxes of ice cream every Friday night for any family members who decided to come. For a family that eschewed most other vices—drinking, smoking, long hours in front of the television—this was a weekly sugar-fest, where two, three, and if you counted the thin sugar cookies, even four helpings were permissible. The weekly event took on mythological proportions for those who lived too far to come. They could only dream of the thin, flaky crusts, the sweet filling made of berries Betts picked in summer and froze just for this.

"I'm always glad when they come around," Betts said, getting up as I gathered my things to go back to my room for a while. "Sometimes nobody comes. But most times, we have somebody. I like to make the pies. It gives me something to do. I made apple for tonight. Grandpop peeled the apples. Oh, I know he doesn't like to do that, but he does it anyway."

"I'd rather sleep," Henry said.

Betts pointed a finger at him. "Yeah. But it's good for ya to do some work."

"Like I say," Henry agreed, "anything that isn't used deteriorates."

10

Under the
Whole Heaven

My depression was a kind of internal bleeding. A rupture of the soul. While I was still living in New York, and for a time in Pennsylvania, my dreams filled with wars, wounded people, blood. Maybe I'd seen too many Vietnam movies that year. Or too much Gulf War coverage. Whatever the cause, the effects were theatrical. I hated to go to bed, and when I finally did, I couldn't sleep. Jonathan, when I was with Jonathan, hated how much I hated going to bed. It was terrible for our love life.

One night, while I was living with Eleanor in New York, sleeping—or not sleeping—on my thin mattress on the floor, I had my requisite nightmare. But this one was different. This one had words. A little girl had drowned, and there was blood in the water around her. I was in the water, too, and someone was shouting down at me from a boat: "It's your body! Reclaim your body!" When I woke up, I felt sick. I knew this was some message that I was supposed to get. But I couldn't understand it. I had no idea what I was supposed to reclaim. I had lost something—my sanity? But I already knew that.

Living on the Hill, I talked to my mom a lot. Talking with her was like talking with God, only with my mom I got answers. My mother has a strong faith and a strong optimism, and reconnecting with her was like reconnecting with a part of myself that I had forgotten. I, too, had been buoyant at one time. My determination to be independent in college had put distance between my parents and me, but in being near my mom again, I started feeling like her way of being would eventually rub off on me, like yellow pollen. It would happen. It had to.

The images I have of my childhood are like a funhouse mirror. There are things that look absolutely idyllic—like making candles and pottery with Mom, building forts in the woods with my sister, singing songs around a campfire with my dad playing guitar. There are lots and lots of playmates. But there are warped parts, too—the scary rapture movies, dreams about going to hell, begging God to forgive me over and over and over. And that one moment after school, when I was sure I was left behind for all eternity.

One night midwinter, I convened a "talk" with both of my parents, something I'd never done before. My father and I had not been close since I was a teenager. I couldn't separate him from the religious tradition he represented for me. I couldn't even separate him from the God I saw him as being spokesperson for. After all, he had been my minister as well as my father. So I had conveniently put my dad, my tradition, and God all together in one box and shoved them way back on some mental closet shelf. Melvin and I had been working hard on locating this box. Now it was time to unpack it.

When we talked in their living room—in Pennsylvania, only a half hour from Bally—I told my dad I was struggling with aspects of my childhood. He was bighearted, filling in details I couldn't remember about how he related to me. He apologized for the times he was critical of me. We talked about how hard it was to separate him from his role as a minister, with the church starting in our living room as it had, then moving only to the other side of a flimsy wooden door next to the couch. I acknowledged that I saw him more as a minister than my dad.

We hugged, and it felt weird, letting my dad in on my life. But good weird. And it was good weird, too, when after we talked I noticed his face had changed. It was just like that moment with my grandfather, when I saw him for who he was. I hadn't really looked at my father's face before—I mean really looked at him. He had lines on his face, and his beard had a lot of gray in it. When I went back to my apartment, I cried for all of the years I'd kept him in that little box on the shelf. I'd thought it was all his fault that we weren't close.

At my next session with Melvin, when I told him about my conversation with my dad, he looked like he was going to get up and dance the mambo. He said I showed great progress—I was bringing the work we were doing into my relationships. I felt like a kid, lapping up his approval, happy to have an angel like Melvin on my side.

◆

Henry was in his forties and critically ill from an infection caused by strep throat (in the days before penicillin) when he had the chance to meet the other side. He was lying in his hospital bed when he found himself approaching a city emanating colors and sounds that he'd never experienced before on earth. People were approaching him, and one of them he recognized as his mother, whom he had never met. He was about to cross over to them, but Henry was hesitant.

"What about the twins?" he asked them. At the time, Roy and Ray were the youngest of four children. To his relief, a voice told him that he would be able to stay until they were grown. Having conveyed their message, the welcoming committee vanished along with their immortal city, and Henry eventually got well.

It was one of several such revelations into other dimensions for Henry. There was the time in his sixties when he was in the hospital for a gall-bladder operation. My mother's dad Ellis, an ordained minister, prayed not for Henry's gallbladder but his back pain. At the time, my mother wondered if Ellis knew what he was talking about. But Henry later wrote this to his children:

> Bally, PA Sun eve Oct 27, 1974
> Dear Folks,
> Greetings of love from home. . . . The past week was as usual, nothing of vast importance happened. So I guess that brings us up to date.
>
> I would like to share my experience in the hospital. It stirs my emotions and brings tears to my eyes as I think about it. It was so real, personal and holy I hesitate to publicize it. I did share it with Mother and wanted to share with you when we were out, but couldn't.
>
> As I felt myself getting weaker every day and could not sleep, I saw as it were the great white throne at a distance. The Father and the Son descended and were conversing together and were going to send for me, but they were waiting for the Holy Spirit, their representative on the earth. And I saw him coming with the prayers of the saints, and when they met, the Father & Son & Spirit agreed to answer the prayers for my recovery. As I was completely at peace I accepted their decision. But they said I should go through much suffering, which I did. Others will never know how much. As I see it, at any age especially for an older person who is ready, why pray for recovery when to be with Jesus is far better.
>
> At the same time I saw, as we say sometimes, a prayer chain. It seemed every prayer was a link in a chain in the form of a triangle and as the last prayer closed the triangle, immediately I was healed. Praise his name. I praise him over & over again. We had 3 sessions of meetings today and no backache. Now you may say, this is not the scriptural way, maybe not, but it is as I saw it.
>
> The Sunday before Al had for his sermon, Job, and the devil said through Job's wife, curse God and die. He also came to me and said if there is a God why should you suffer so. If there is a God why does he not answer

the prayers of the churches at Boyertown, Levittown, Salem, Goshen, Bernside Fellowship. . . . When I was the lowest, a card came in the mail. In it was a small plastic cup with a grain of mustard seed. The sender will never know what it did for me. I kept that on top of the pile.

Nuff said for now, Dad

◆

My grandfather's experiences intrigued and miffed me at the same time. My own experience seemed so shallow by comparison. Why didn't I get any directives from angels? I felt I had missed the mark somewhere. And because there was no one else to blame, I shook my fist at God for not being trustworthy and at my family for not conveying better the path to enlightenment. It was the end of the year, December, and the storm outside fed my discontent. It was raining torrents and thundering like a hundred drums, a storm out of its season. I was trying to write, but couldn't focus, angry that after all of the personal work I was doing, my marriage might still be over. I was pissed off that my depression seemed to swing away and crash back in at will. My friend Melanie, who would understand the most, having tried to do away with herself the year before, was across the globe visiting family. We sent each other letters, and I'd tried to figure out how I could join her there, but I had no money, and wouldn't be getting any anytime soon.

Tearing my papers from the typewriter and throwing them across the floor, I cursed God in the thunder rumbling outside my window. Even if God wasn't there, because I wasn't really sure if God was, I was angry at fate, the whole freak cosmological accident of existence. I wanted to attain the greater spiritual connection that Henry had as proof that I wasn't alone. I wanted to be on that path to nirvana that Henry seemed to tread with ease and that I had lost so many years ago.

I accused the flashes of lightening out the window, "You're a deserter! You think you're so loving. You call this love?"

It felt good to get angry. I'd been reading a book called *Angry Women* about performance artists who expressed rage through their work on stage, and it was freeing to see pictures of women bearing this unfamiliar expression. Save for lots of plate-smashing in New York while Jonathan and I were still under one roof, I had forgotten how satisfying it can be to throw things. It was a way to keep anger from going inward and raiding my psyche. I was a pacifist, learning the basic rules of war.

After the thunder seemed to quiet, and I had paced back and forth enough to wear the carpet thin, I grabbed my pack of cigarettes to go outside for a smoke.

My apartment exited onto the gravel driveway below the house. I was barefoot, hoping the discomfort would wake me up and distract my thoughts that were as pushy as rush hour commuters.

Looking up, I was met with an immense clear sky. The storm had vanished. Stars stretched over the hill, like a giant doily. I found the Milky Way, and breathed in the moist, clean air, forgetting for a moment the reason I had come outside. I stood looking up for a long time at the celestial bodies burning in the cool water of space. I stood there for several minutes, until I sensed a slight movement, a vibration. Like a breath, as if God, if there was a God, was breathing. I took a breath, too, a deep breath, and found it hard to hold onto my anger, with so much space before me. I found the Big Dipper, and imagined a God that immense to be able to use a cup that big, slurping up the heavens.

Once when I was a teenager, something happened that was so unexpected and intense that I hadn't ever told anyone about it. Under that starry Bally sky, it came back to me.

I was at a Jesus rally with my church youth group and had picked up some bad lower back pain along the way. The Jesus rallies I attended in the early 1980s were a mixture of Christian music concerts, pep talks, and prayer vigils, held under large white canvas tents or on makeshift stages and which lasted for several days. I was sitting with my group around a fire at our campsite, which was one of several hundred sites sprawled across a field where water pumps and port-a-johns served as the only provisions. We'd had a jam-packed day and were regrouping for the night. It was common in this kind of setting to ask for prayer for one thing or another, and it was so routine that I asked for prayer for my back, not counting on any answer. But as we stood there, holding hands around the fire, my friends taking turns praying out loud, a curious thing happened.

A flame, or what felt like heat from a flame, seemed to ignite at the base of my spine, and travel upward, spreading outward as it moved. When it reached my middle back, it was so intense that I thought I would throw up. I took a deep breath, trying to steady myself, unsure of what was happening. The flame moved higher yet, up through my neck. I was still holding the hands of the people next to me, still standing, but wondering how long I could stay in this position before I'd collapse. Then, just as quickly as it came, the flame was gone, leaving only remnants of the heat it had generated in my body.

It had happened in less than a minute. For the remainder of the prayer time, I tried to get my bearings, uncertain of what had just happened to me. I scanned my body, looking for pain, and there was none. My body felt loose and warm.

I'd heard of people being healed at rallies, of such radical things like someone's short leg growing longer to match their normal leg, or someone in a wheelchair standing up and walking, but I never took that to be real. What happened to me around the campfire was real. I had had pain, then came the flame, then the pain was gone.

After the circle broke, the youth group leader came up and asked how my back was. I said casually, "Oh, it's feeling a little better, thanks." I couldn't look him in the eye.

Under the stars, after the storm over Kulp Hill had passed, it seemed there was some parallel: I had knocked and received an unexpected answer—then for my back, now for my life. It was as if some presence—God, the cosmos, the energy between the stars—had been simply waiting for me to pay attention.

I looked up at the sky for so long I developed a kink in my neck. I smoked my cigarette, and turned in for the night.

That night, Clyde and I curled up on my bed in our usual configuration: I slept on my side, and Clyde wedged into the half-moon space created by my bent legs.

In the odd way your mind takes your reality into your sleep and messes with it, I dreamed I was chasing a big cat—a cheetah. I was tracking it in sand all the way to New York City and beyond. I was tired but kept running and running, until I came to a bunch of tall grass. It was a surprise to see the grass on a stretch of sand. Even stranger was that I recognized it as Rousseau's painting, *The Dream*, which I'd seen at a New York museum. I heard someone calling. "Stop!" the voice was saying. "Stop!"

I went into the grass, which was full of creatures, and behind there was a great lion lying on the sand. Without thought, I laid down on the belly of the lion. We lay there, belly to belly, and the sensation of peace was so strong it obliterated any sense of borders or boundaries. I had never felt such a thing in my conscious or unconscious life. It was a serenity that had nothing to do with desire or pursuit. The specificity of place and personhood—the outline of things—was completely gone. There was a feeling of love and completeness, without the vacuous feeling of things unfulfilled. This sense of peace started far beyond me, went through me, and continued into oblivion. The space surrounding us was filled with the peace I felt. I stayed there within that eternal space for a long time, the kind of time that happens when you are about to have a car accident, you see it coming, how everything is drawn out, lasting absolutely forever. Except there was no death here, no edges, no grief. Only eternal, expansive love.

When I awoke, I couldn't believe I was back in my finite skin. Clyde was stretching in the new light.

"Why?" I asked the daylight. "Why did I wake up?" *But dummy,* I thought, *You'd be dead.*

I realized, with a sudden lightness to my body, that this was a new notion—not wanting to be dead. I sat for a while on my bed, trying to hold onto the sensation of the dream. I felt light, buoyant as a cloud, but it was fading. I pulled out my journal and wrote down everything I could remember.

I'd been reading Job, the poor fellow who in a series of disasters lost everything he owned and everyone he loved except for a few misguided friends. Maybe, I thought, as was the case for Job, this communiqué uncovered the great purpose of it all, depending on how you look at it: down on your luck, about to call it quits, you find the Supreme Being letting you in on a secret, a game that's been going on. It's Russian roulette of sorts that has to do with what you lose and what you keep. Maybe it's your family you lose, or your possessions. Maybe it's your job, or maybe your sanity is up for grabs. Whatever it is, it is out of your control, and it will make you PAY ATTENTION.

I pulled out Job again, to the page marked with a torn shred of paper, and read: HAVE YOU ARMS LIKE GOD'S? CAN YOUR VOICE THUNDER LIKE THAT?

My family kept their channels to the divine open through regular prayer. Melvin believed dreams were detailed messages from God. I still didn't know what I believed, except that I'd been invited into an eternal realm that made everything I was worried about—my marriage, my writing project, my future— look less like a fumbling and idiotic performance on the brief stage of life, but an important (if complicated and messy) part in a grand eternal play.

Clyde brushed against my leg as I was journaling and I reached down to pet him. He had cataracts in his eyes and looked at me through the filmy gray substance. I wondered what he dreamt about last night.

11

Electric

*J*anuary came like an unwelcome guest. Christmas festivities with my family were over; the dark winter months promised no resolution for my marriage. I'd been on the Hill far longer than expected and wasn't sure what to do with myself next. I didn't want to set up shop in a new apartment, in a new town, only to have to pack it all up if Jonathan returned and we went back to New York. So I was in limbo and getting cranky about it.

After the holidays, a letter came from Jonathan, post-marked in Damascus, Syria. His plans were, he explained, to travel to Sudan to visit his cousin, Keith, who lived there and after that, go to India, a trek he estimated to take another six months. It was the kind of letter that gave me hope and clawed grooves in my heart all at once. But I was getting used to this.

He wrote that "my return and our reacquaintance will address our doubts. I hope you can understand that, even though I love you & want to work things out, I have to wait until my return when we're together before I can be confident about how you feel toward me. I think you can understand this in light of how unsuspecting, surprised I was w/ your feelings of empti-ness toward me when we broke up. . . . "

I sat down on my sofa and stared out through my tears at the gray clouds, the bare trees. I was doubtful about the stability of my feelings toward him as well, but I had to trust myself. During these months on the Hill, I was feeling more love for him but also something far more solid. I was gaining a love for myself.

◆

Knowing I had six months to go and potentially much longer before I could hope for any resolution, I sat on my sofa and began to brainstorm about where I wanted to live. Although my friends lived in New York, I found the city over-stimulating and now full of bad memories. I thought of more manageable cities where I knew people: Portland, San Francisco, Seattle. The pro and con list I was making became messier and messier as I scribbled around the edges, not focusing well. I wadded up the paper, and threw it at the brick wall across from my sofa. It hit the wall lightly, and fell silently to the floor.

I decided to talk to my aunt and uncle. They'd invited me to dinner and listened quietly while I told them about Jonathan's India plans. The future's uncertainty seemed to follow me like a loyal dog with foul-smelling breath, and I wondered if they were beginning to smell it, too. But loyalty is strong in my family, and they offered for me to stay the remainder of the year. I asked them if they were sure. I was a quiet guest, but I also knew about that three-day smelly fish rule that I'd broken, oh so long ago. They gave me an unhesitating yes.

So here I was, becoming a permanent fixture on the Hill, like a flowering annual that has forgotten to die at the end of the season. For something different, I visited Henry's shop with him. His wooden shed was situated several hundred feet from the house, next to the pen for Ginger, my aunt and uncle's aging pony. Henry's shed looked like a cross between a shed and a boat, since he had installed a glass wash machine window to the shed's door, giving it the look of a porthole. As we passed Ginger's pen, the pony came over expectantly. Betts often wrapped up her dinner rolls at restaurants to feed to the pony when she got home, but that was her ritual, not Henry's. He patted Ginger on the nose, and we went together into his shop.

On the inside of the shed's door were his myriad of plaques. One near the top said, "Come in, we were expecting you—everything is going wrong today." Beyond the door were drawers upon drawers of screws, nuts, bolts, tools, oil cans, pocket knives. It was all neatly ordered. Henry was quiet as he showed me around. He rearranged some tools and, in search of a certain screwdriver, opened a cabinet revealing a secondary universe in which tools were lined up in neat rows like an orchestra.

One couldn't say Henry loved to talk about his work because he wasn't one to talk, period. But in talking with him about his work, I noticed a certain glimmer in his eyes and a lilt to his voice that wasn't often there.

Back at their apartment, Betts busied herself cleaning the kitchen, while Henry and I talked in the living room.

"Longacre—that would've been my brother-in-law—Longacre had a little electrical shop in Bally," Henry said finally, swiveling a little. "I started there in 1934. We used to set electric light plants in the homes. Then you would make your own electric with a little gasoline engine and a generator. Only 32 volts. It wouldn't power an electric iron. Later they made them in 110 volts, and you could use a wash machine.

"There was a farm outside of Clayton I remember we wired for electric. As the electric extended farther and farther, we just followed the line.

"Setting electric light plants, we'd go pretty far from home. Longacre used to take me to the Deep Run area, and I'd stay overnight. He'd drive home and fetch materials for the next

> Nov. 23, 1943. Made some ribbon bows and ironed a big wash. Henry was home for dinner. He was wiring Leonards' cellar and ran down over the fields for dinner.

day, so I could keep on working. Most were Mennonite homes, and they would provide a meal and lodging. Of course, I wouldn't put in the plants on a Sunday. I'd be afraid lightning would strike!"

At the same time I was laughing, I was filing the story away in a mental cabinet labeled, "Principles I won't live up to."

"We started wiring electric refrigerators to sell," Henry continued, folding his hands over his waist. "And electric washers. All kinds of electrical equipment. Longacre came up with the slogan, "We service what we sell." He sent me to Philadelphia to learn how to repair refrigerators. Many of the department stores would sell them, but they wouldn't have anyone to fix them. So we had plenty of work."

He looked at Betts, who had sat down to join us.

"Don't look at me, or I'll talk," Betts said.

His smile to her told me he was happy for this chance to take the stage, uninterrupted and undisturbed.

"Longacre sold a refrigerator," Henry continued, "to a woman who lived in town. She complained it wasn't working properly. So I went to look after her refrigerator. She said, 'There isn't any ice in the ice trays.' I asked, 'Did you fill them?' She said, 'No, I guess I forgot.' 'Well,' I said, 'you'll have to fill them!'" Henry paused, laughing in his quiet way. 'Don't tell anybody,' she said. And I didn't tell anybody as long as she lived."

"Nobody?" I asked, skeptical. Of course, he'd at least tell Betts to amuse her.

"I didn't tell anybody."

I tried to imagine this, the day of her funeral, Henry finally telling the one about the woman who thought the ice was supposed to appear like a genie out of the empty freezer. It was a great story about machinery and belief. How we are so unaware about how a machine performs its particular function, that we are willing to believe anything is possible.

I asked what it was like working in people's homes.

"You can learn from younger people," Henry added. "You can learn things that we old people don't even think about. Take for instance, I repaired a lot of refrigerators, and for that you'd have to get on your knees. And there'd be youngsters there. I didn't allow them to play with my tools, but sometimes they'd ask me questions. 'Why do you use this tool? Why don't you use this?' And sometimes I'd learn things from youngsters that as an old experienced man I didn't even think of."

Betts couldn't help herself and interjected, "Henry would take our boys along when he worked for Longacre, if he'd go away evenings to a job. Remember? You used to go where Alfred Detweiler had electrical work for you. And the children always wanted to go along there because he used to give them such big plates of ice-cream to eat."

Henry adjusted his wristwatch. "Yes, that's right," he answered.

We took a break for pretzels and coffee in the kitchen. The cold seemed to seep through the walls, even though the heat was on. I cupped my coffee between my hands, until we got back to the sofa, where I picked up my pencil again. I was always taking notes, even with the tape recorder, because I, unlike my grandfather, didn't trust machines.

"It was during the war that you quit Longacre," Betts said, back in the living room. She was referring to World War II.

"See," he explained, "you had to have priority to buy materials. Longacre couldn't get materials. They couldn't get priority because the government thought it wasn't necessary."

"Longacre couldn't buy a refrigerator," Betts said. "He couldn't even buy repair items nor wire for wiring houses. Everything went to the military, you know. They used it for the war."

April 14, 1945. Most of the stores were closed today on account of the services for Roosevelt and the grocery stores were closed part of the day.

"So then I went to Bally Case and Cooler," Henry explained. "They needed an electrician there. And they paid sixty cents an hour—so it was an improvement. 'Now,' you'll say, 'how did Bally Case get materials that were rationed?' They made wheel hubs at that time. It wasn't direct government work, but they could get materials because of that."

The clocks chimed two o'clock.

Henry continued, "There was a man I worked alongside at Bally Case. Gus was his name. Gus was quite a fellow. His vocabulary was not *please*, not *thank you*, not *good morning*. I'd say, 'Good morning, Gus.' His greeting was, 'Huh.'"

I'd heard stories about this nemesis from my dad. Gus was the maintenance supervisor and Henry was the electrical foreman in the same department.

"The boss and I got along well together, and Gus was jealous. He'd do anything to irritate people. Gus told me once, 'Don't cross my pipes with your wires or I'll rip 'em off.' One day he was no different than the next. But of course I had to cross his pipes with the wires, and he couldn't do anything but curse."

"He'd get to you," Betts said, glancing at Henry. "Every once in a while, you'd bring your tools home, and say you'd quit. But then you'd cool off, and go back in."

Henry nodded. "He was sore because I got along with the boss, and he was for the union. I didn't think you'd need a union if you could just talk to the boss directly."

Aunt June's husband, Nelson, worked with Henry at the same place. She told me later something Henry never would've told me himself. When Henry would be working on a ladder, Nelson said, Gus would always shake it when he walked by, just to get on Henry's nerves. One day, Henry decided that he'd had enough. Standing on his ladder, he noticed Gus approaching and so he perfectly timed a wad of spit to land on Gus as he reached out his hand for the edge. Henry's projectile was perfectly aimed. Gus never shook Henry's ladder again.

"In the morning," Henry continued, "I'd go down at seven o'clock and check in. There are a lot of things that you do in a place like that which go beyond the call of duty. Often on a holiday or a weekend, I'd go down to the plant and listen to the wiring. In those days, if there was something wrong, you could hear it. And if you found something wrong, you could fix it.

"Then new machinery came in with more elaborate controls. It came to the place where I'd have had to go to school to learn to fix these things. I had enough to do with just the ordinary electrical stuff. I said, 'I can't handle more.' I said we'll have to get somebody who understands electronics—computers, you know. So Stanley, he more or less took over the electronic stuff. I kept responsible for the other.

"When I quit, I was seventy-two. I didn't expect to live this long." He paused to look at Betts, who was nearly asleep, propping her head up with her hand under her chin. She nodded her head in agreement. They talked about their travels with Betts' sister Ruth, and her husband Andy, who led bus tours across the United States.

"If I could've got a part-time job, I'd have gone back," Henry concluded.

Henry stopped talking, and Betts brightened when I asked if we should call it a day. As much as we enjoyed these sessions, we also looked forward to when they were over, and we could just talk about nothing in particular, like the weather.

Betts put her hands on the ends of her armrests to get up.

"I should'a made lunch for ya," she said.

"Oh, no" I said. "You do that enough." I knew it was time to go. For her "lunch" meant actually going through the trouble

---

July 24, 1945. This eve. Daddy and Henry Paul went with the Bally Gospel Gleaners to Allentown State Hospital to give a program for the CPS men working there.

of making a stew, a roast, a pie, or something complicated. I gathered my things, went back to my room, and grabbed a yogurt from my apartment refrigerator.

◆

Having introduced the idea, Betts invited me for lunch later that week. We sat around their white Formica table, the table that reminded me of their old kitchen, the one that now belonged to Aunt Sandi and Uncle Roy. In that kitchen, I played hide-and-seek with cousins, plucked candy and licorice from cabinets, played checkers with my grandmother, and gathered other such memories that gave the kitchen table a set of mysterious powers, such as the ability to make me feel both small and secure, and hungry for pot pie all at once.

Now that Henry had begun talking, he was like one of those old Fords you needed to crank to start—once he got going, he was pretty reliable.

Over slices of pork roast, he recalled, "In the Sixties Henry Paul's were doing mission work in Cuba, and we wanted to go visit. Well, we needed a passport. So, I sent my two dollars to Harrisburg, and they replied, 'You can't get a passport.' I drove out to Harrisburg. I looked at their records. They showed me their library. There they had their book of the census. And in the official book under Yoder were Nelson, Norman, Edna, and Verna, but no Henry.

"I argued with them. I said, 'Now look. A Henry Yoder has been paying taxes since 1935.' I said, 'Where is he? I want to meet him.'"

"'We don't know. We have no record of a Henry Yoder.'"

"'Well,' I said, 'If I claim I'm Henry Yoder, here I stand. Now you say I wasn't born?' I don't know if I said it kindly, but I didn't feel kindly. They admitted that in 1906 there was a record of a child in the home of Henry Yoder [Sr.]. 'And,' they suggested, 'that may have been you.' 'Well,' I said, 'Here I stand.'"

I kidded him, "Maybe you were never born."

"Yes, I just grew up as a weed."

Betts saw that I'd finished my pork and said, holding the platter out to me, "Don't ya want some more?"

◆

Henry and Betts were increasingly becoming "real" to me, like a pair of Velveteen Rabbits. I'd made all kinds of assumptions about their perfection as the family elders, and those assumptions were being worn away. Things didn't always work out the way they'd planned. Hearing how their lives went made my own situation seem less freakish—sometimes life just twisted and turned on its own merry course, and you had to keep up some how. I was learning from Henry and Betts that the best thing you could do was to live each day in the best way you knew. I was trying that on—living each day for that day, and not for the future. It was a sort of Zen experiment. I jogged, I wrote, I had conversations. That was my day. My husband was far away, but the day, taken for itself, wasn't all that bad. Especially now that the sky in my mind was clear in a way it hadn't been for many years.

My grandparents, as long as I can remember, had a ritual of sitting on the front lawn of my Great Aunt Ruth's house and watching the colors change over Butter Valley as the sun went down. The view goes on for miles: over houses, tavern, the Catholic chapel, over the farms and wooded hills, over the red brick house where Henry was born. After dinner, one evening in early spring, when it was not yet balmy but we were anxious to begin the ritual again, we pulled out the lounge chairs from the garage, and traipsed up the flagstone steps to the front lawn. Last summer we'd sat there, Betts and I shelling the final crop of

> Oct. 11, 1945. Did some sewing. Made myself ten aprons and finished a dress out of feed bags.

limas from her garden into bowls. And last fall, we'd put on sweaters and listened to the cicadas calling and answering.

Now the trees were still naked, but birds were singing tentatively, and early buds were on the maple tree behind Aunt Sandi and Uncle Roy's house. It was the maple tree with leathery bark, in whose shade we held summer family gatherings.

Two cars passed in succession. Henry remarked, "There's more traffic coming up the Hill nowadays."

"This isn't traffic," I said.

"Oh, no, not after you lived in that city," Betts said, and I had to smile. "That city" meant a place beyond her understanding or interest. It was the same for computers: she called them "that thing."

Henry leaned forward on his cane, which he pinched between his knees. He had stumbled a little on his way up the steps from his apartment, and caught himself with it. I'd always thought it was an aesthetic thing: he collected canes. Even though he dressed simply, he did maintain a certain dapper togetherness that was enhanced by the cane. But today it struck me how frail and elderly he really was.

"Now, about the golf course down here," Henry said, poking his cane toward the view. "That was the Gehman farm, where we lived in the Thirties. That used to be my grandfather's farm, you see. And I've always thought that if Grandpa Gehman could look down he'd say, 'Here's the old tree where we had the mailbox hung on, and this looks like my farm. But what are they doing, batting little balls around the fields?' When you think of it that way, it's kind of a sorry use of the landscape."

"Not for golfers," I added, as a devil's advocate.

"It's a way to make a living," Betts said.

"I remember the sledding we used to do there," Henry said. "We would go all the way up to County Line. There we could start. Across the cornfields, we used to go *click, click, click*—the cornstalks breaking when we'd go over them with our sled.

"I don't know," he mused. "That's all I remember. That's one of the reasons I didn't want to grow old. People become childish when they get old. You can't remember things. You can't act right. You stumble around."

After a while, Aunt Sandi and Uncle Roy appeared with their chairs, and we rearranged ourselves to make a sort of semi-circle facing the valley.

"Well," my aunt said. "We finally can sit out." Her tone accused winter for lasting too long.

Talk turned to plantings: what plants would be bought at what greenhouses, and how Zern's was having a good special on pansies. I was starting to feel less uncomfortable with them, more part of the scenery, like a stone settling into its place on a wall. The night crept cool onto our backs from the woods above. In summer, fireflies emerge in the field across the road, the same field I pummeled with bare feet as a child, picking bluebottles for my Grammie. Now, there was only the anticipation, the waiting. Still, the air smelled of lilacs, as it always did, even before their season.

A man in a green sedan drove by slowly, honking. We all lifted our hands and waved.

Nov. 11, 1945. We were at Perkiomenville this morning. Harold was baptized. We had a little lunch along and then went to Towamencin where A. J. Metzler preached on "Strong Men and Beautiful Women."

12

Peace Offerings

*I*t was the end of February when Jonathan called. I couldn't believe how much his voice sounded like the voice I remembered from college, soft and seductive, as if he'd practiced for the call.

"How are you?" I asked. "Where are you?"

"I'm in Egypt. Look, we can't talk long, but I wanted to say that I'm coming home soon."

I held my breath, hardly believing what he was saying.

"I hope we can try to work on things," he said.

"I thought you were going to India," I said cautiously.

"That would mean end of summer before I got back, and I'm thinking that might be too hard on us."

"Well—yes."

I was surprised that this was a consideration for him. "When will you come back?"

"I'm thinking April. I hooked up with some people here, and we're going to see the pyramids. . . . "

"Okay, okay," I said, cutting him off. I didn't want to hear about his travels, the things he was seeing to get away from me.

"I'm hoping you'll want to move back with me to New York again. Maybe we could live together or apart, whatever works."

I hadn't thought that far ahead. As much as I wanted to be with him, I hadn't thought about logistics.

"Well, we'll talk about that, okay?"

"Okay, just think about it."

"I'm glad you're not going to India. I really miss you. I love you."

"I love you, too." The words felt strange in my ears, as though heard through water.

Then we hung up. I looked at the calendar. February 23. I had over a month to go.

I invited my friend, John, to visit. John is a poet and paper-maker who taught speech in a cleared-out nurse's office next to the closet where I had taught English as a second language the year before. He had split with his fiancé the same spring Jonathan and I were falling apart, so we had commiserated to-gether. He's of Scottish descent, and I was never sure in talking with him if I was hearing a brogue or a New Jersey accent, prob-ably both. In any case, between his soft voice and gentle man-nerisms, he's like a teddy bear in Bleecker Street clothing.

It never occurred to me that there would be any problem with him visiting. We went together for pie night at my grand-parents' place, and I introduced him to my grandparents. Betts immediately offered him a seat on the sofa next to her chair. This was a place of honor, a seat beside the matriarch, where a visitor is pummeled with questions and made to feel like he or she is the most interesting person to have been born since Ein-stein. Before I could sit down, my grandmother was already asking John about his work as a teacher, and the conversation went rolling along as sleek as a red wagon.

Then one of my aunts came through the door, knocking and entering without waiting to be invited in, as is the custom with my family.

I stood up to introduce John, and the slightest wrinkle ap-peared on my aunt's brow. It was such a slight wrinkle that I could have misread it, but I don't think I did. It was a look of bewilderment. I had been concerned about John seeming too off-the-cuff New York, and I'd completely forgotten that he was male and that I was separated. A woman just didn't invite a man to her place when her husband was away—not ever, under any circumstance, let alone under these circumstances.

Though they never play poker, my family is great at poker faces. My aunt shook his hand cordially, and the conversation went back to teaching. It was an odd juxtaposition—John sitting on my grandmother's davenport, leaning against the afghan, in black leather biker's jacket and with hoop earrings. But when the lemon pie was served, he cooed over it, which made Betts smile and say condescending things about her baking. This meant she'd taken the compliment to heart.

Later, John and I sat in my chilly, basement apartment exchanging writings. I read his lyrical poems, and he read parts of my oral history. Then our writing led us to other subjects.

"Are you going to wait for him?" John asked. I wondered if he thought waiting showed a sign of weakness or desperation.

"He called. He said he's coming back in April. Besides, I'm not just waiting for him," I said. "I'm doing my own thing."

"Yeah, this is incredible. You're really fortunate, you know, in some respects. You've got a great family."

I was surprised by his comment and mumbled some "Yeah, that's true" response. It was nice to see that through his eyes. Of course I loved my family, but I wondered if others would see them as a little too sunny, which is how I saw everyone on my bad days. And I did have bad days, though they were less frequent and came with fewer sinister spirit sightings.

"I'm glad you think so," I added.

John was planning on staying overnight, and in New York, he would have crashed on my floor, but my aunt asked if she should offer him a room upstairs, and he wisely accepted.

The next day, John asked if I was coming back to New York. We were sitting at a red-checkered table at the Bally Hotel.

"I don't know, John," I replied, pained to think I would lose my favorite niches: the dollar theater, Summer Stage, Symphony Space. But I was starting to like the serenity of the country. I liked spotting raccoons in the woods.

He nodded, taking a swig from his beer. I missed John and Eleanor and my other friends. I missed going to bars without wondering if anyone had seen me. I felt a vertigo of my two worlds wobbling on opposite ends of a delicately balanced beam. On one side were my free-spirited writer friends, who were my lifeline, anchoring me in the world. On the other hand was my conservative family, anchoring me to a connection with the spiritual world, with the seasons, and with my history. I wished the two worlds would mingle, and I could be more myself around my family. But I was afraid. One wrong move, and there would be bruised sensibilities everywhere. At least that was the assumption I lived by that kept me scuttling from one side to the other over the rickety bridge of my psyche.

◆

A week later, I boarded a Greyhound bus headed for Tennessee to see my closest girlhood friend. Ingrid picked me up at the bus station, and we drove to her country house on a small sloping hill. Ingrid didn't look much different than she had as a teenager. Petite with long and full black hair, she has absorbing ebony eyes that tease and invite you at the same time.

I had never been to Tennessee, and I wasn't prepared for the lush beauty of the Appalachian foothills, the long distances between houses. I met her husband, Jim, for the first time, and her four children, her ten-year-old Danny reminding me of Ingrid's brother, how he looked at you from his charcoal eyes and tufts of black hair as if through many thoughts.

While baby Tessa bounced in a swing like she was preparing for takeoff, we ate biscuits and gravy that Ingrid had prepared. Jim was from the north, too, but his grandparents lived in Tennessee. Their town offered a life outside the rat race—a slower, more greenish existence. Still, there was an intensity about Jim that shone through his starry blue eyes. He was a mason, and I imagined him burning holes in the bricks with those eyes.

The next day, we sat in Ingrid's living room, talking about the yellow jacket incident and revisiting our family comparisons.

"You know," she said, feeding pureed carrots to baby Tessa, who was trying to grab the spoon away and spread the meal on her clothing. "I always thought your family was the bright and shining example. You were like the Brady Bunch."

Three-year-old Tara and six-year-old Jessica were playing Barbies in one of the bedrooms and were running in and out, giggling.

"I thought you were more free," I retorted. "I mean, I know your dad hit you, but you didn't have as many rules and regulations as I did."

"Oh, we had rules."

"Yeah, but I had the social pressure to be the good girl of the church."

"Okay, so we're even."

Then Ingrid remarked at how stubborn I used to be, and I told her "Look who's talking," and we laughed, and the ten years that had passed since I'd seen her last were gone in one twirl.

We were just back from a trip to waterfalls in the Appalachian Mountains, when the phone rang. Ingrid picked it up, and said it was my dad, handing me the phone with a quizzical look.

"I have some bad news," he said.

Jessica, who was five, was sitting on my lap. I'd been playing with her hair that was long and black and shiny like Ingrid's.

"Okay," I said, "I'm sitting down."

"Edna's mom had another heart attack," he said. This was my mom's mom, my Grammie Mack, the one I could have been spending a year with except that her depression and my own made that scenario less likely. She was the Grammie I wished I knew better but didn't, feeling that she and I had something in common. I didn't know why she was depressed, in the same way I didn't know the source of my own malaise. But I also knew that depression often comes without reason, a chemical stew in the brain whose ingredients are not always discernable.

"She didn't make it through this one," my dad said.

I braided and unbraided Jessica's hair, while she watched my face and I talked about getting there for the funeral. He said there was a big snow coming, and I'd have to leave immediately to make the funeral in time. I let go of Jessica's braid to hand the phone back to Ingrid.

Ingrid had visited my grandparents' farm when we were kids, so we talked about the things we associated with her: playing with her porcelain dolls in the attic, making applesauce in the yard, plucking grapes off the arbor and sucking out the juice. We talked until it was time to gather my things. In the kitchen, where we ate a small meal before we left for the bus station, three-year-old Tara saw that I was upset, and was trying to puzzle this out like a hole in a favorite blanket. She asked in her small voice, "Your grandma died?"

"Yes," I said.

"And you didn't want her to die?"

"No, I didn't want her to die."

Ingrid's whole family gave me a ride to the bus station. Behind the rope barrier, they waved good-bye as I boarded the bus. Even Tessa waved her pudgy arm. I gathered this image close to me—my childhood friend, in the safe arms of adulthood.

The snow was already starting, and it was coming down in a fury of flakes. I stared out the window, while the white petals of snow filled the horizon.

My Grammie Mack was a serene and quiet woman for whom depression came in her retirement years. She had huge, blueberry eyes that looked like she could see right through you to another realm. I wondered if she took in too much, perhaps because that's how I felt. I didn't know—as some people seemed to know—how to diffuse it, or let it roll away, or breathe it out, or whatever other people do with the grit of life. I knew what it was like to be trapped inside my own body, to feel like others would never know how hard it was to simply get out of bed sometimes. I don't know if this was the way she felt, but I imagined she felt that way.

Of course, she had suffered things I knew nothing about. Her first child, and only son Paul, had died of pneumonia. They'd buried him on his first birthday. Some years later, a hurricane tore off the roof of the farmhouse, and some years after that, the barn burned. It must have been a hard life for her, with the constant demands of the farm, raising five girls while my grandfather was busy with the fields, the cows, and his work as a minister of their church. I'd wanted to ask her what her life was like. But now it was too late.

When the sun went down in Virginia, we were the only vehicle on the road. Our bus driver stopped every mile or so to bang the ice off of the windshield wipers. Finally, after our windshield had turned into an iceberg that couldn't be conquered, the driver announced that we'd be staying the night at a middle school until the roads were cleared. Everyone groaned.

The exit ramp was full of ditched cars.

At the shelter, which was bustling with Red Cross volunteers and stranded motorists eating chicken noodle soup, I called home. My dad told me that the funeral would be postponed a day because of the storm. And there was other news: my sister, Juanita, who was expecting, had gone into labor.

The ride home the next day, I felt like Alice in Wonderland. Everything had been transformed into a white bag of confectioners' sugar. I stared out the window at the smooth drifts, thinking about Grammie.

When I arrived at my parents' house late that night, they told me that Juanita's baby had arrived. It had been a difficult labor—the chord was around his neck—but they'd pulled him out in time. They'd named him Nicholas Thoreau. Birth and death came together, a double screen where one passes and one arrives. I wondered if their souls passed each other on the way.

My mother wanted as many women involved in the service as possible, and I was chosen as one of the pallbearers. The weight of it was more than I'd imagined, carrying my grandmother's body through the shoveled path to the grave. As we stood around the casket suspended over the hole in the ground, I made a promise. I vowed that I would do everything I could to live freely. This was my one opportunity to be on this side, in this skin, and be in it well. I was a woman with many choices and opportunities, more than she would have ever dreamed of having, and I would take advantage of what was offered to me. I imagined my grandmother in her afterlife, taking off with eagle's wings, rising, high above the old stone church, looking back for only an instant before she lifted up beyond the treetops. There was no question in my mind that she was free now.

Under a flapping green tent, we sang a song as the casket lowered. When the minister had finished his prayer of committal, and people started dispersing to the funeral meal, one of my aunts pointed out Paul's little grave marker nearby.

"She's at home with Paul now," she said.

♦

I knew Jonathan would be home in a few weeks or maybe a month, but every moment seemed to stretch out like Gumby. I couldn't reach Jonathan to tell him about my grandmother's death. And even if I could, I didn't think he'd be a good shoulder to cry on. We weren't that for each other any more.

So I jogged every day, pounding the pavement to jostle away the grief that clung to my body like putty. I realized one morning, though, jogging up the Hill, that even though I was grieving, something was different. I was jogging instead of drinking, I was crying instead of trying to put on a good face for the world, and I felt connected to the people and events around me. I even felt connected to my grandmother, who was now deceased, but in me somehow, like a potion.

The next time I saw my mother, she gave me the black, wool sweater my Grammie Mack used to wear. I put it on, and it was like having her arms around me. It would be my symbol for the promise I'd made to be free, to seize all of the opportunities available to me. When I took the sweater off that evening in my apartment, I hung it on the back of my writing chair.

◆

It was a week later, a Friday night, and I'd joined my family for pie night as usual. Death makes you notice things more. Like how your breath goes before you as you walk in the cold air. Or the thud of your heavy boots on the wooden steps. After pie night, I walked toward my apartment holding a leftover cheesecake, thinking I'd spend the night reading. It was yet another empty night, after a long year of empty nights. I had my typewriter and the cat. I had books, and letters from Jonathan. I had the stars, and a slice of moon. I was getting used to this emptiness, had come to expect it.

When I rounded the house, I stopped in my tracks. There was a backpack lying in the middle of the lighted driveway, but no one with it. I went closer, thinking it was Jonathan's, but also thinking about how my uncle was a pastor and how it could be just anyone looking for a place to stay. On top of it was a large, hand-scribbled sign: "Bally." I crouched down and opened the zipper. I found beaten leather sandals, a scruffy notebook. It was Jonathan's, I felt sure. I stood up and looked around.

"Jonathan?" I called into the darkness. No one answered.

I called again.

"Hi," a voice said quietly, from the region of the back deck.

I spun around to see a bushy-looking man leaning against the wooden rail of the stairs. I barely recognized him through his mass of facial hair. The last time I'd seen him he was stripped of all hair from head and face, like a jailbird. He came down the steps, and we wrapped our arms around each other.

We stayed like that for a long time.

"Wow! I can't believe it's you," I said, stepping back. I can't believe it's *you*."

"Touché, then."

"Can we go inside?"

"Yeah—it's freezing out here."

He picked up his backpack, and we went in through the door that served as the front door to my room. We made small talk, sitting across from each other, he on my writing chair, me on the sofa. Then he opened his backpack and pulled out a lump of clothes. He stripped away one item after another, until he came to a hard surface. He pulled out a ceramic drum.

"It's from Egypt. You can see it as a peace offering."

I thanked him and mumbled something about a cool gift, still bewildered at the night turning on its head as it was.

I gave him the leftover cheese pie and went in search of a fork. I found a plastic one on top of my refrigerator.

"You hitchhiked?" I asked, returning to the sofa.

He took the fork and dove into the pie. I wondered when he ate last, if he was hungry. He looked thinner than usual, and he had already started out thin. Then I thought maybe I'd been hanging out with my grandmother too long.

"Yeah, I wanted to surprise you and didn't have a way to get here from the bus station," he said, resting the plate on his bony knee. His jeans were worn and pale, frayed at the bottom. "This car passed me going the opposite direction, then he turned around and came back. He was a teenager, a really nice guy."

I was surprised someone picked him up at all, looking the way he did. "He was going the opposite direction?" I asked.

"Mm-hmm," he replied.

I tried out the drum.

"You said you needed something to bang on, so I thought you might like it."

It had a deep, echoing sound. It was true that I needed something to bang on. When we were splitting up, I'd broken too many plates. This would make a loud noise, and I'd still have dinnerware in the morning.

"Yeah, it's great," I said. "So where's you're tent?"

"I shipped it home. It was too heavy to lug around."

"Yeah, I bet." I didn't want to talk about his travels. I wanted to know what was next.

"Great pie," he said.

Then he said he couldn't stay long—he had to leave the next day, in fact, to catch up with his sister and brother in Pennsylvania, his other sister in Baltimore, and also some friends in New York.

"Maybe we can meet with Melvin again," I offered, trying to stomach his leaving again, after he'd just arrived.

"Yeah, I was thinking we should, too."

He started talking about something that happened to him in Jordan, but I cut him off.

"Can we just not talk about Jordan for now?"

"Okay, sure. I don't have to talk about it. What do you want to talk about?"

"Us."

Then he came to sit by me on the sofa, close enough for a kiss. I wondered about his facial hair. If he was planning on shaving it at some point.

13

Up the Hill

We were washing dishes in the kitchen after dinner Sunday. Jonathan was with his family in Lancaster. He was planning to return soon so we could have some sessions with Melvin and talk about our future. We were going to give it another go, we'd decided, but we had some edges to smooth out, places where the fabric was too frayed for us to jump right back into things.

Henry's hands were immersed in soapy water, and I was drying. I wondered how my life was going to change.

Betts was putting the leftovers into plastic containers. "My mother died seven days after I was born," Henry said. "I think I've told you that before."

I nodded, and put the plate I'd been drying back into the cupboard above me.

He continued, "I always felt there was something missing—up till school age. Then I don't know if it was a dream or a vision: I saw my mother in Glory. No one had told me what she looked like, and we didn't have pictures, but there she was with brown curly hair and wire-rim glasses. A pretty young woman, about twenty-four."

He paused and turned to me. I was rinsing the dishes, and I stopped, too. He'd had so many visions. I wondered if he felt different. Open, maybe, like a broken piece of pottery.

"I don't know why the wire-rim glasses. I guess so many people wear glasses. After that, I felt that I had found . . . well, I felt satisfied."

"You got to meet your mother," I said.

Henry stepped back to inspect the floor, and tapped the rug with his shoe. "Do you know why they call these throw rugs? The tendency is, they want to throw you."

He always had a poetic element to him.

He placed a dish gently in the rinse bowl and continued, "My brother Nelson's wife passed away this year, and I had an audience with the Death Angel. 'Well,' I said, 'It's nice you could take her to Glory.' He said, Yes, and I'm coming back for you.'"

I was drying another plate, and I gripped it tighter.

"Oh, no," I protested, but Henry didn't seem perturbed by the idea.

"With him," Henry said, "it's a different feeling or atmosphere. It's hard to describe. When you enter the heavenlies, there's a certain peace. I don't know if that's the English word you'd use, but it feels like peace."

I nodded, trying to dry my plate again.

"So when he comes, and there's judgment, and he separates the good and the bad, I trust I won't be found sinless, but maybe faultless before God. So I look for the time that the Angel will come for me."

Henry emptied the dishwater, and said pointedly, "There's a time to wash dishes, and a time to stop washing dishes."

"Yes," I answered. "I guess that's true."

I put my plate in the cupboard, his words lingering like a disturbing dream.

◆

Nov. 12, 1946. A beautiful day, very changeable.

On a picnic table that I could see through the bay window, Betts had her pots of spring flowers: narcissus, yellow and purple pansies. A white Easter lily bloomed on the bay window sill, brought by one of their children. Its aroma filled the room. I felt like a painter, seeing finally how the colors and shapes of my family balanced each other out. How my grandmother's talkativeness met with my grandfather's silences. How his wry humor met with her laughter. How she was disturbed by small things that showed his age, wanting to hold onto him forever. How he welcomed death, a path to the familiar. He saw visions of the heavenlies, and she gathered her family around—her earthly saints.

Betts had already made her chocolate coconut Easter eggs, and she gave me a handful for my apartment refrigerator.

There was so much territory to cover yet, but there would always be more material. They had, after all, each lived eighty some years. That was a collective one hundred and sixty. I knew this might be our last formal meeting for the oral history project. I was ready for the next thing and getting restless—*schusslich,* as Betts would say.

Still, things moved more slowly than I wanted them to.

Today we sat in the living room, and Henry confided, "There was a time I developed hiccups for a week. Even at night, the body would fall asleep, but the hiccups didn't stop."

The body, he said. My maternal grandfather, Ellis, also spoke of his own body this way, as if it were not his. "The hand." "The foot."

Betts looked up at him from her work on a needlepoint runner.

Henry went on, "I remember that different people prayed for me, and it just didn't stop. And we used all the common ways of doing things—taking a teaspoon of sugar, taking a mouthful of water, holding my breath. Whatever old-fashioned thing they'd recommend, we tried it. The nurses brought ideas from their homes, and I just kept on hiccuping."

"What did you do then?"

"The boss at Bally Case had a doctor who recommended getting coca cola syrup. I took a spoonful of that. The same day, this young fellow from church, he came to pray for me. And the hiccups stopped. Now I wonder sometimes. Who should get the credit? See?"

"There are things that you think about," Henry said, rubbing his hand across his cheek, "when you just sit here in a rocking chair and you stare into space. Especially when you can't see well. I can see a rocking chair or sofa, a television, a mixer, and everything. I can see it, but it's fuzzy. It's not clear. You take life today. I just live one day at a time, which the rest of you do, too. Take it as it comes, and try to look on the good side of things. Be thankful I can see enough that I'm not stumbling around all the time. That I'm able to care for myself. I can still wash myself. Still shave when necessary, which is daily."

"You can still tell stories," I offered.

"Still tell stories. Tell stories that are fit to be told," he replied, with a small chuckle.

"How do you feel, Grammie?" I asked. "What do you think about?"

"I think things these days are going a little too fast," she said, laying her work down on her lap. "I don't know where they'll end. In this computer age, people don't want to use their heads any more. Everything has to be done mechanical."

"Man's heart hasn't changed," Henry added, "but the way we do things has changed—now is it better or worse? I don't know. As far as people are concerned, a lot of things are better, but their relationship to God—it's worse."

"They say we can do things without God," Betts said, "we don't need him, but in the end we do."

April 9, 1947. I worked in the factory again but I think that will be my last day there.

Henry shifted in his chair. "My philosophy has always been," he said, "if you don't like something the way it is, then change it. Is this world better since we lived here? All these years we lived here, did we improve anything? I'm not sure."

My grandmother shot him a look, frowning. "It isn't for me to say," she said. "Maybe we did some good, but not as much as we should've. You can never do too much good."

Betts brought out the photos of their anniversary celebration, coming to sit next to me on the sofa.

There was the cake-cutting and the presents, their kiss after the clinked glasses.

She handed one photo to Henry, exclaiming, "Ach, Henry, see this photo. Look how bald I'm getting!"

Henry smiled his half smile and replied, without missing a beat, "You can't have hair and brains both."

14

The Eastern Gate

Henry and Betts had made arrangements. It suited them, two people who had believed in a God and an afterlife for so long. It was their own special ending, their own private rendezvous. It gave them something to look forward to, a beginning of a life, not an end. Even if you don't believe it, maybe you're a little like me and have a weakness for fairy tales.

Along with choosing what burial plot, what suit, what dress, what minister, what favorite hymns, they also designated a spot where they'd meet again, in the afterlife. Whoever journeyed first to heaven agreed to wait at the entrance for the other. In company of the cherubim and seraphim, Henry—as it turned out to be—would wait, leaning against the Eastern Gate, like a midnight lover, until his darling Betts appeared.

Henry had a major stroke three years after I left the Hill. When he was transported from the hospital to a retirement community to receive care, my uncle Roy asked him if he was okay with where he was going. Henry shook his head no. The very next morning, Henry drew his last breath.

Shortly after Henry's death, I gave Betts a version of this book, which she kept by her reading chair for the next four years. In early November 2000, I received what I can only describe as a communiqué. I was sitting in the dark, meditating, when the message came that it was time for Betts to go. I burst into tears, shaking my head in refusal. But Betts was ninety-one. She missed Henry terribly. I knew I had to let her go.

Three weeks later, only days after she'd convened her family for a traditional pig stomach Thanksgiving dinner, Betts had a stroke. My parents and several of my aunts and uncles were with her in the hospital when she died. Uncle Roy described her passing this way: she was breathing slowly and raspily. Then all at once her mouth dropped open. She raised her head slightly, as though she had seen the most amazing sight. Then she laid her head back down and was gone.

◆

Jonathan and I moved back to New York City several months after his return. There was a shift in our relationship. I was more balanced, for one. And through the process of breaking up (and seeing Melvin, a.k.a. the angel), we'd learned how to fight. We didn't throw plates as during those last days of our break-up, but we could put our feelings out there for each other, whether thick or thin or thorny. Our year of pain ended with a summer of exploring swimming holes in Bally, and biking on Nantucket. We'd paid the troll, and now we could eat the green grass. To commemorate our "new" marriage, we bought wedding bands. (Being Mennonite, rings weren't in our tradition, but the earrings we'd exchanged at our wedding had been stashed in a drawer long ago.)

When Jonathan and I decided to create our own family, we named our son Gabriel for the miracle he was. He was born with black curls, the tips tinged red as if he'd been out in the sun. Betts had two-and-a-half cake-filled years to dote on him before she passed on. The last time I spoke with her, it was on the day of her stroke, after she'd already lost many of her words. I told her that I loved her. "Yes," she said, "And the little one."

◆

I still return to the Hill on occasion to visit and to buy pottery from Uncle Roy's pottery studio, which now takes up the entire basement, including the apartment where I once stayed. And I return often in my mind. When I do this, I sit under the maple tree, the one behind Uncle Roy and Aunt Sandi's house, where Henry and Betts convened many summer gatherings.

When I do go there, the tree is always thick with green, rustling leaves, its trunk leathery, a great, aged torso. I am alone, because the gathering has ended, and some have gone inside or home, taking leftover string beans and pie. Only the voices echo under the tree, as if the leaves themselves hold the words that were spoken and whisper them back to me—not specific words, but the essence of the words, like the notes of an old familiar song. I stand there listening to the tree, the one I have known since earliest memory, accepting the emptiness, knowing my grandparents are with me but not with me.

If I have time I go down into the basement where I lived during that year. While there, I enter a dream I had one night in spring, before Jonathan returned, before we began the work of being together again. And in that dream, the self that was worn out and in pain is a disheveled body in rags, hung up on a meat hook in a corner, dead. And the self that is new, learning what it is to live again, is a woman in repose, emerging out of a crack in the earth, as if from the crater of a volcano. She rises with no support but sheer energy. As she does, the energy surrounds her and I see that her skin is smooth and shining out the warmth of the sun, and that her hair is long and flowing like the wind.

Sometimes, when I don't know where my life is taking me, and I feel like the fragments won't hold, I think about this dream, and that tree, and its leaves singing their music. I remember that I've come from someplace that is rooted in the earth, and a people who bathe their tears with dreams and gardens and song. And underneath it all is a spring whose cherry-wine water you can drink with a tin cup.

Sometimes, that is all I need.

Recipes from Betts' Kitchen

LENT AND EASTER RECIPES

Fastnacht

These doughnuts are made on Fastnacht Day, the Tuesday before Lent. Traditionally, they were to use up any excess fat in the house before the Lenten season of fasting. Betts made them throughout the year.

Ingredients

1 cup warm water
4 packets active dry yeast
3 cups reconstituted milk or warm water
1 cup sugar
4 tsp. salt
4 eggs, whisked
1 cup soft shortening or margarine or vegetable oil
14 cups unbleached flour
Confectioners' sugar for coating the Fastnacht

Dissolve yeast in 1 cup warm water. In a large bowl, dissolve the sugar in 3 cups warm water or milk. Add to the

Prayer Before Meals

We thank Thee, Lord,
for this our food;
God is love, God is love.
But most of all for Jesus' blood;
God is love, God is love.
These mercies bless,
and grant that we
May live and feast
and reign with Thee,
May live and feast
and reign with Thee,
God is love, God is love.
Amen

sugar/water mixture the melted shortening, salt, and whisked eggs. Then add the yeast. Whisk gently together. To this, add the flour, 1 cup at a time, using a large wire whisk. When the dough starts getting stiff, use a heavy wooden spoon. Dump onto floured board and knead for 10 minutes, adding a dusting of flour frequently to prevent sticking.

When kneaded, place in a large bowl and cover with a towel. Let rise for one hour, then punch down with flour-dusted fists. Let it rise again for another hour, then punch down again. Roll out on the board and cut with doughnut-shaped pastry cutters dusted with flour.

In a frying pan, heat the one cup of fat to 380 degrees. Cut open a brown paper bag and spread out on counter for draining the fried doughnuts. Place doughnut raised side down into oil, using a fork to lower it in. Fry until medium brown on under-side. Then flip gently, using a fork. Brown the second side and then remove with two forks onto brown paper to drain.

Shake in a paper bag of confectioners' sugar or eat plain.

Chocolate Easter Eggs

Betts kept a box of these in the refrigerator for guests at Easter time.

Ingredients
3 fresh coconuts
3-6 lbs. Confectioners' sugar
2-lbs. chunk of bitter chocolate
2 tbs. (1 tbs. per pound of chocolate) cooking wax

Preparing the Coconut

Cut hole into coconuts. Drain out juice. You can drink this or discard it, depending on your taste for it. Pry coconut from the shell and peel off the brown skin. Grate or grind the co-conut pieces with a meat grinder or food processor.

The Eggs

With your hands, mix sugar into the grated coconut. Squeeze the sugar and coconut together. Mix very well, for

about 30 minutes. Form into oblong eggs, about1/2" x 1 1/2."
Set on wax paper and cool in refrigerator, 24-48 hours.

For the next step, you'll need a double boiler, or a heat-proof bowl set in a sauce pan. Heat water in the boiler or pan, and place the chocolate and cooking wax in the upper boiler or bowl and stir until melted. Insert a toothpick into an egg from the top and dip into chocolate quickly, coating entire egg. Let drip over the bowl and return to wax paper. Refrigerate.

THANKSGIVING

Dutch Goose

The familiar name for Dutch Goose is "Pig Stomach," referring to the membrane in which this dish is cooked. Betts served it at Thanksgiving with applesauce and pickled cabbage, and pumpkin pie for dessert. Serves 6-8.

Ingredients
3 lbs. cubed pork loin or pork roast, about 1/2" thick
3-4 lbs. cubed potatoes
Salt and pepper to taste
Pork stomach membrane (ask your butcher)
1/2 cup browned butter
You'll also need: white thread, a large plastic cooking bag, and an aluminum pie plate that fits into your boiler.

Preparing the Goose
Soak the stomach membrane in a salt/water mixture for several hours ahead of time. If membrane has more than one main hole for stuffing, sew the extra hole(s) shut with white thread. Mix the potatoes and pork in a large bowl, and spoon it into the membrane pouch. When filled, sew the opening shut, and place the stuffed pouch into a large-size Reynolds cooking bag. At the top of the Reynolds bag, cut several 2" slits for air to escape.

In large boiler, fit aluminum pie plate at bottom to prevent burning. Place filled bag into boiler and add enough water to come up 1" over sides of stuffed pouch. Quickly bring to a boil. Reduce heat to med/low (so that water keeps bubbling, but not a rolling boil) and maintain (covered) for 3 hours.

Getting It Out of the Pot

With pot holder, hold the Reynolds bag with contents over boiler and cut a slit in bottom of the bag to drain off any excess liquid. Getting the bag out of the boiler can be a tricky job. It's easier if you have someone near to lend a hand.

Remove from boiler to a large serving platter. Remove plastic cooking bag and discard. Cut into strips 2" wide. Drizzle browned butter over it to serve.

Pickled Cabbage

A fine side dish to Dutch Goose

Ingredients

4 cups grated cabbage

1/2 cup finely chopped green pepper

4 tbs. sugar

4 tbs. vinegar

1 tsp. salt

Stir ingredients together and serve.

CHRISTMAS

Bavarian Cream

Bavarian Cream is served at Christmas to top off a feast of ham, oyster filling, and green beans. Although the dessert is delicious by itself, Betts served it alongside mincemeat pie.

Ingredients
2 cups milk
3 eggs
1 cup whipping cream
1/3 cup cold water
1/2 cup sugar
1 envelope Knox gelatin
1 tsp. vanilla
Soak gelatin in cold water in large bowl. Set aside.

In a saucepan, stir yolks of eggs into milk, and cook on low, stirring constantly, until it coats the back of a spoon. DO NOT let the mixture come to a boil or it will curdle and that will be the end of your cream. Remove from heat and add sugar and vanilla. Stir into gelatin mixture so that the gelatin dissolves completely, and let it cool until almost gelled or set.

When mixture is nearly set, in separate bowls whip the cream and the egg whites. Gently fold these into the gelled milk mixture. Refrigerate until ready to serve.

BREAKFAST CAKES

AP's Cake

AP's Cake is a stiff cake often dunked into coffee at breakfast. The name "AP" are the initials of the woman who originally sold this type of cake at a Philadelphia area market.

Have ready: two greased 9" pie plates
Ingredients
3 cups flour

1/2 cup sugar
1 cup brown sugar
1 tsp. baking soda
1 tsp. baking powder
3/4 cup margarine or butter
1/2 cup milk (more or less)

Mix all the dry ingredients together. Then cut in the margarine or butter with a pastry blender or fork. Add the milk slowly, mixing thoroughly with a large, heavy spoon. Add less milk if you want a drier cake. Don't handle more than to just mix it together. Dough will look much like pie dough and be quite stiff. Press the dough into two generously greased 9" pie plates. Sprinkle a little flour on top of each pie and press down slightly with a flat hand to level the dough. Flower your knuckles and knuckle down the top to give some texture. Bake at 350 degrees, for 25-30 minutes.

"This cake's greatest attribute is that it only gets harder and better as it sleeps because the harder it gets the more it needs to be dunked in the coffee, which we all know is the best way to enjoy it!"—Uncle Henry Paul

Shoofly Pie

This is a breakfast cake or dessert. Betts served it both ways. It's so sweet, you'll have to shoo away more than flies.

Have ready: one 9" pie pastry

Ingredients

Filling

About 3/4 cup molasses: mix together 1/4 c. Dutch Barrel Molasses; 1/4 c. Mrs. Shlorer's Golden Table Syrup; 1/4 c. Black Strap Molasses
3/4 cup boiling water
1/2 tsp. baking soda

Crumbs for topping

1/2 cup whole wheat flour
1 cup unbleached flour

1/4 cup Crisco
1/2 cup brown sugar
Dissolve the baking soda in the hot water. Mix in the molasses with a wire whisk. Set aside.

In a bowl, combine sugar and flour. Rub in the shortening with a pastry blender or fork to make crumbs.

The pie is created through layering the contents of these two bowls in just the right proportions.

Dust your unbaked pie shell lightly with flour. With a measuring cup, pour 1 cup of the liquid onto the bottom. Then take a handful of the crumb mixture, and sprinkle the crumbs over liquid until you can't see any liquid. Next, pour 1/8 cup of the liquid gently from the center, making a spiral over the crumbs. Dust lightly with crumbs, once again covering the liquid, especially covering the edges to prevent boiling over. Alternate in this way, making sure you reserve enough crumbs to finish on top.

Bake at 375 degrees for about 40 minutes. This recipe should give you a crumb layer on top, a cake-like center, and a gooey bottom.

FOR SOMEONE WHO'S BEEN AWAY

Pot Pie with Homemade Noodles
Betts made this for family members she hadn't seen for a while. Serves 6-8.

Ingredients
The Dough
1 cup of flour
1 egg
2 1/2 tbs. milk or water
1/2 tsp. salt
Stir the egg with no more than 1/4 cup of milk or water.
Mix in flour and salt.
Mix the dough together with a heavy fork or your hands,

until you have a thick, gummy glob, and it begins to come away from the bowl. When mixed, let it sit in the bowl, covered with a towel, for 20 minutes or so.

Roll out on a board, to 1/8" thick. Cut into squares, 1 1/2" a side. Use lots of flour so they don't stick.

The Stew

In a Dutch Oven or 4-quart boiler, in 1 quart of water, cook a 2-3 lb. chuck roast or chicken for several hours until tender. Remove the meat from the bones, and keep separate from the broth.

Peel and cut up into quarters: 2-3 pounds of potatoes. Place in lightly salted water, so they don't brown, and set aside.

Bring the broth to a boil, and add the potatoes and the squares of noodles to the broth. Return the pieces of chuck or chicken to the pot, and add salt and pepper to taste. Reduce to simmer and time for 30 minutes. Chopped parsley is a nice addition at the very end. Serve with pickled cabbage and homemade applesauce.

Notes on Diary Entries

1. Traditionally, most Mennonite women wore head coverings weekdays and Sundays. Betts, like many women in her generation, wore a bonnet—a rounded, dark-colored cap—when outdoors and a white, mesh covering when indoors.

2. Betts made a hot sweet-and-sour dressing, poured it over uncooked, young dandelion leaves, and topped it with hard-boiled eggs and bacon pieces or sausage. She served it with mashed potatoes.

3. "Thirds" is the batch of socks passed over for "seconds." Over ten years, Betts mended and paired some forty thousand Gold Toe socks from the Bally Knitting Mill, which were taken by her church, Boyertown Mennonite, to homeless men at the Bowery Mission in New York City. "Sometimes I'd have as many as fifty socks without a partner," Betts said. "I'd send them up anyway. Maybe somebody would wear them without a match. You know, one of our grandsons—I won't say who—never matches his socks. He just pulls two out of the drawer and puts them on. I guess that's all right with him, not?"

A Note
About Mennonites

*M*ennonites are multicultural, multilingual, even urban. The stuff of Pennsylvania Dutch Mennonite culture has to be seen simply as one slice of a greater Mennonite pie. This can get tricky. On the one extreme, Mennonites have strong roots, whereby early followers in Germany and Switzerland were martyred for insisting on baptizing adults instead of infants.

Mennonites hid, ran for their lives, moved to other countries to escape being hung, burned at the stake, or tortured and imprisoned. Mennonites left their families and countries of origin to cross the Atlantic, sometimes not making it, to an unknown wilderness where they'd at least have religious freedom and live out their belief in peaceful nonresistance.

That said, this all took place in the seventeenth and eighteenth centuries. Hiding from the world isn't a matter of life or death anymore. This brings us to the other extreme, when the Amish broke away from the Mennonites in the nineteenth century because they thought Mennonites were *too worldly*.

By the twentieth century, Mennonite churches split and coagulated into groups: some donned plain, black clothes, and kept to themselves; others grew tired of these trappings and traded their plain coats in when cheap leisure suits became a better buy. These later churches tended to diversify. So now, you might meet a Mennonite and mistake her for Amish, or you might meet a Mennonite who has a nose ring and who's shaved his head and lives on Avenue D. Either one, though, would give you an opinion on peacemaking.

Photograph Captions

The Beginning
    1. Cynthia Yoder, New York City
    2. Jonathan Shenk

When I Was a Boy
    Henry, on left, with his brothers, Nelson and Norman

The Minister's Daughter
    Betts and her friends

How Did We Get Along?
    Henry and Betts. Inset: Out with friends.

A Fair Trade
    The Yoder store in Allentown, Pennsylvania

Red-Hot Pokers
    1. Henry on his scooter with grandson, Allan.
    2. Henry with the twins, Roy and Ray.
    3. Betts and Henry with sons Henry Paul, Roy, Ray, and Harold.

4. *Top:* Betts with twins, Roy and Ray. *Bottom left:* Henry and Betts' five sons: Henry Paul, and Harold (back), Roy, Arlin Richard, and Ray. *Bottom right*: June, Henry and Betts' only daughter.

Electric
1. The stuff of Henry's shop.
2. Rich, the youngest son, moves a cabinet of Henry's tools.
Photos by Juanita Yoder Kauffman.

Up the Hill
1. Betts in her garden.
2. Henry and Betts, 1992. *Photo by the author.*

Recipes from Betts' Kitchen
Betts rolls the dough for steamed strawberry pudding. *Photo by Juanita Yoder Kauffman*

Back cover and page 188
Photos of author are by Joyce Heisen.

Acknowledgments

I remember my grandparents for their generous spirits. They welcomed me without question into their daily lives and participated in this project. I learned so much from them—and still do from their enduring spirits.

I thank my parents, Ray Yoder and Edna Mack Yoder, for their love and support, especially during the year this book elucidates. I also thank Edna for helping with recipes, as Betts never wrote them down, and Ray for penning the "Prayer Before Meals."

Uncle Roy and Aunt Sandi Yoder opened their home to me, lent an ear when an ear was needed, and let me tie up their phone. Without them, collecting these stories would have been a much more difficult task. I will never forget their generosity.

Eleanor Levine and Dan Shenk also came to the rescue at a critical time, and I'm eternally grateful to them for their compassion.

I thank the following writing mentors for their sparkle and for their perspectives on this work: Barbara Probst Solomon, Kate Knapp Johnson, and Lucie Brock-Broido. Friends have been my north star. I thank the following writers: Ann Cefola, Gwendolen Gross, John Currie, Kaydi Johnson, Chris Conroy, Maud Lindsey, Mary Alice Rocks, and Melissa Stabler. For their input on the earliest draft, I am grateful to Haven Colgate, Adrienne Laws, Linda Scott, Mary Thomas, Andrea Yost, William Bryant Logan, Peggy Harrington, and Jay Wegman. I also thank Donald Beckwith.

I admire Ingrid's and Annamarie Milano's courage and openness. I thank them for being part of my story, both written and unwritten.

Family members helped with this project in so many ways. They are a blessing. Sandi Yoder, Tonya Yoder, Anita Yoder, and June Yoder Shenk wrote down recipes. June, her husband Nelson, and my other uncles—Rich Yoder, Roy Yoder, Harold Yoder, and Henry Paul Yoder—helped clarify facts and fictions and added a few of their own. My brother-in-law Kenneth Kauffman was a perceptive reader as well as brainstormer over the book title. I am grateful to David Yoder for introducing me to Millen Brand's work, and to Grace Yoder Gehman for her own memoir.

I remember Abe Schmitt for his acts of kindness. His words remain in my heart. I thank John Kavanaugh for his coaching.

Part of this work was completed while a graduate student at Sarah Lawrence College, and I thank Mickie Eschweiler and the P.E.O. Sisterhood for their interest in my work and their financial support. I also thank the Women in Communications group of the Westchester Community Foundation for their recognition of my work and financial contribution.

I'm honored by those whose efforts helped bring the book into published life. John L. Ruth took time away from his own writing schedule to write the Foreword. He is also responsible for preserving the diaries of some of my forebears with the Mennonite Historians of Eastern Pennsylvania. He is a beacon, and I thank him. I am also indebted to Michael A. King, the publisher of this book. I am especially grateful for Michael's generosity, his care, and his spirit.

I also thank Gwen Stamm for her care in creating the cover and Bob Blosser for his technical skill. Paul Schrock deserves many praises for his insightful editing. Beth Grossman is an extraordinary publicist, advisor, and friend. She and my business coach, Christopher Flett, and right-hand woman Lora Friedman, are sudden angels.

My friend Ben Stutzman has my devotion for putting his zany energy and creativity into developing the website, www.cynthiayoder.com, where this book is promoted.

Finally, my sister Juanita Yoder Kauffman provided illustrations for this book, not to mention heaps of encouragement along the way, and I owe her great thanks. She's a luminous companion. Of course, this book wouldn't have been possible in its present form without the unwavering support of my husband, Jonathan Shenk. He is moonbeam.

I thank these individuals and all of my family and friends for supporting me in ways beyond which I've described. Their lives have brightened my path, and by extension, this story. And to you, dear reader: I bow to the light in you.

The Author

*C*ynthia Yoder has worked as a journalist and teacher and holds a Master of Fine Arts in Fiction Writing from Sarah Lawrence College. Her creative nonfiction and poetry have appeared in national literary publications, including *Parabola, Cortland Review,* and *Lumina.*

Yoder earned her B.A. from Goshen College, a Mennonite college in Indiana. Moving to New York City, she studied literature at Columbia University and taught at a Lower East Side elementary school. In 1992, she moved back to eastern Pennsylvania to begin writing the stories that appear in *Crazy Quilt.*

Yoder lives in New Jersey, where she works as a freelance writer and participates in Friends (Quaker) Meeting. She lives with her husband, Jonathan Shenk, and their son Gabriel.